My Nest Isn't Empty,

It Just Has More Closet Space

Also by Lisa Scottoline

My Nest Isn't Empty,
It Just Has More Closet Space

The Amazing Adventures of an Ordinary Woman

Lisa Scottoline

AND

Francesca Scottoline Serritella

ST. MARTIN'S PRESS NEW YORK

www.stmartins.com

Photographs on pages 14, 24, 53, 91, 110, and 111 by April Narby.
Photographs on pages 113 and 116 by Joanne Donato.
All other photos courtesy of the authors.

ISBN 978-0-312-66229-5

First Edition: November 2010

10 9 8 7 6 5 4 3 2 1

For Mother Mary

Contents

~~~~~~~~

My Nest Isn't Empty,
It Just Has More Closet Space

A Woman At The Wheel

It all begins with Nancy Drew.

And it might end there, too.

I grew up with a girl crush on Nancy Drew, and it came back to me recently, when I was organizing my books at home. I found a few of the Nancy Drew books I had as a child, among them the blue-thatched copy of *The Mystery at the Ski Jump*. It's even older than I am, copyrighted in 1952.

My copyright is 1955.

As a girl, I not only read the Nancy Drew books, I memorized them. I identified with her, although we had nothing in common. She was rich, I wasn't. She was slim, I wasn't. She had a distant father and no mother. I was close to my father, and I had Mother Mary.

Who's enough mother for both of us.

Nevertheless I loved her and I still do, even in my fifties. Could there be two times in a woman's life during which she feels like Nancy Drew—pre-puberty and post-menopause?

Possible.

But why, for me?

For starters, Nancy's blond, and I'm blond in my mind.

She has a dog, and I have five dogs.

She drives a convertible roadster, and I drive an SUV.

Well, they're both cars.

Plus we both have a boyfriend. Hers is Ned Nickerson, and mine is George Clooney.

Finally, we're both on our own, which enables us to have all manner of adventures. And kidding aside, that's at the heart of Nancy Drew. That she's free, and in charge of her own fate.

No one is telling her what to do. No mom, dad, or hubby. No one can. She doesn't ask permission. She hops into that convertible and drives.

Fast.

Nancy Drew was an ordinary girl, who was extraordinary in so many ways, and because of her, I started to write novels in which ordinary women were the heroes, because we're all extraordinary in so many ways. I'm talking teachers, lawyers, journalists, at-home moms, secretaries, painters, accountants, and nurses.

In other words, you and me.

The novels became bestsellers, thanks to you, and the trademark Scottoline heroine is Nancy Drew with a mortgage, or how I feel on a good hair day.

It seemed only natural to segue from writing about fictional extraordinary women to writing about the real extraordinary women in my life, though it's a new experience for me, in some ways. In a novel, I have 100,000 words to tell a story. In one of these vignettes, I have 700.

I can barely say hello in 700 words.

I'm Italian.

Also, in a novel, I'm writing fiction, and here, it's real life. The characters in this book are my family and friends.

Even though they're still total characters.

Inside you'll meet Daughter Francesca, who writes on her own in these pages, spilling all our family secrets, like when she tells me what to wear on a blind date.

Hint: Show the wares.

And you'll read about Mother Mary, the feistiest octogenarian on the planet, who lives with Brother Frank in Miami. And my late father, Frank. Sadly, he has passed, but he's here, too.

That's how it is when we lose our parents, or anyone we love.

They're passed, but always present.

As for my pals, I'm closer than ever to best friend Franca, and as you will read, I spend Christmas Day with her and Meryl Streep. And you'll meet assistant Laura, who sets me straight on having 700 people to my house for a book club party.

You'll even get to know my array of two cats and five dogs, including a new puppy that makes me wonder if I'm becoming an animal hoarder.

Answer: Possibly.

By the way, I'm divorced twice, from Thing One and Thing Two, and they hardly appear at all in this book.

Why?

They're farther and farther away in my rear-view mirror.

They're so small, they hardly matter anymore.

This happens when we drive, and it tells you I'm moving ahead.

Finally.

There was a previous book about all of these people, but you don't have to read it to enjoy this one. You'll catch on soon enough. I bet because they remind you of the people in your own family.

And your life.

And yourself.

Because I think that women are basically the same, under the hood.

That's why Nancy Drew lives on.

Her life is still all of our lives, as ordinary extraordinary women. Even if we have hubbies and kids and moms and dads, at bottom, we're on our own. Each of us lives her own life, at the end of the day. Each of us has her own adventures, and each of us solves her own mysteries, of all sorts.

Parenthood is only one of the adventures in our lives.

Childbirth is another.

Love remains one of our greatest mysteries.

Marriage, a mystery I have yet to solve.

Nancy may find *The Hidden Staircase,* but we find The Hidden Calories. We may not solve *The Case of the Missing Clock,* but we've all solved The Case of the Missing Sock.

We drive along in our girl convertibles, and we never know where the road will lead us. At every fork, we choose our way, right or left, north or south, not only for us, but for the people we love, in the backseat. We steer a way through this life, for us and our families.

We have a better sense of direction than we think.

Our strength, our wit, and our hearts are more powerful than anybody could ever have imagined.

And even greater than we ever believed.

We are, all of us, women at the wheel.

Hit the gas.

Mrs. Elvis

~~~~~~~~~

I was just asked out on a date.

By Elvis.

For real, kind of. Or, rather, by an Elvis impersonator.

He may have left the building, but he still has a laptop.

He had evidently read somewhere that I'm a huge Elvis fan, which is true, and as he is in the Elvis business, he figured I'd be attracted, so he emailed me and asked me out.

Uh, no.

But, thank you. Thank you very much.

Not that I wasn't tempted, but he didn't give me all the facts, and I wasn't about to ask. Though he did supply a head shot and he looked so handsome—dark hair, long muttonchops, shiny sunglasses—well, you know what he looks like.

I never dated anybody on a stamp.

But he didn't specify which Elvis he was. If he was young Elvis The Pelvis, we could talk. I would make an exception from my no-younger-men rule and become a cougar. Though I'm guessing that this impersonator is pushing 60.

It's an interesting legal question, in a way. If the impersonator is 60, but the Elvis is 22, does that make me a cougar?

Or just a kooky and fun kinda gal?

If he was black-leather Comeback Elvis, I'm still listening. Elvis in black leather on his comeback is my idea of a harmonic convergence. The only way to improve that combination is if he was carrying a big piece of chocolate layer cake.

Don't be cruel.

But if it was Karate-Chop Elvis, I'm less sure. Though come to think of it, maybe I could be talked into it. Elvis is Elvis, even chubby. And I like peanut butter and banana sandwiches. Maybe I shouldn't have said no so quickly.

I'm all shook up.

Still, the very notion of the email opened up new vistas for me, love-wise. By which I mean, if I could start dating impersonators, which one would I date? All of a sudden, I wasn't limited to romance with live men, or even real men.

Wow! It boggles the mind. My odds of finding new love just skyrocketed.

Maybe I was being too picky before, limiting my dating pool to the living. True, the dead can be a little dull, but God knows I've been there before.

The only problem is, if I try to remember long-dead pop stars, I can't think of a single one who does it for me.

I love to listen to Frank Sinatra, but I'm not sure he's my type. Also Mother Mary would never forgive me. She knows they belong together. She longs to be Mrs. Ol' Blue Eyes.

I can't remember any other long-dead pop stars, and the only other singer who really does it for me is Bob Dylan, but he's not dead yet. Though I bet there are tons of people already impersonating him.

Hmm.

Gentlemen, send me an email.

Don't Think Twice, It's All Right.

Hell, come to think of it, I can do a decent Dylan impersonation, so maybe I should start dating myself.

Except I already am.

I wouldn't mind dating an impersonator of historical figures, however. I always had the hots for George Washington.

Chicks dig power.

I could be First Lady, even though I'd be First Dead Lady. I could overlook his wooden teeth, and we could share a blow dryer.

Plus, I had a thing for Robin Hood. I love all that derring-do, with the arrows shooting and the horseback riding, and the helping the poor.

And the codpiece.

What a guy! I would date Robin Hood in a second. I got so excited, I called Daughter Francesca to tell her that her new stepfather would be wearing green tights.

She laughed. "Mom, Robin Hood wasn't real."

"Yes, he was. I saw the movie. In fact, two movies. One with Kevin Costner, and one with Errol Flynn."

"Who?"

"He was real."

"He wasn't."

I considered this. It was possible she was right. She often is, and she sounded it. "But I bet people impersonate him, anyway."

"Maybe."

"So I could date the Robin Hood impersonator. What difference does it make if the person they impersonate is real?"

"You mean like a fake of a fake?"

"Exactly. I could do worse."

"It's a point," Francesca said, hanging up.

Hairy

~~~~~~~~~~~~~~~~

I just found my first gray hair.

On my chin.

I'm trying not to freak.

You should know that I didn't panic the first time I found a gray hair on my head. I coped with it like a mature adult.

I dyed it and went into denial.

But the day you find a gray hair on your chin, your world changes. It's enough to send you back to bed for a few hours. Now I not only have a beard, it's gray.

Maybe I need Just for Men.

Only I'm a woman.

Or at least I used to be.

Now I'm a man with a gray beard. Maybe I need Just for Old Men.

By way of background, it's not the first time I've noticed that I'm growing a beard. It came in about the same time as reading glasses.

Now there's a nice visual. Take a second with that one. Let your imagination run wild.

Those days, I would see a stray chin hair now and then, or at least that was the way I thought of it. Until it filled in nicely and needed trimming.

Suddenly I'm Amish.

Or a billy goat. Or the bearded lady in the circus. And though it's good to change careers, I had other ideas. So I started plucking like crazy.

Which was about the time I started noticing a fine peach fuzz, sprouting all over my cheeks. It wasn't easy to see because it was blond, and God only knows how that happened.

By the time you start growing facial hair, you lose your religion.

Still I was grateful for small favors, and tried to ignore it. But then I started to see more and more peach fuzz, like sideburns, and soon I was sporting full-length girl muttonchops.

As much as I love Elvis, I never wanted to be him.

So then I started plucking like it was going out of style, yanking out these little blond hairs that would look great on a baby chick.

But not on a full-grown chick.

I kept up with it, and at one point, I found myself in a plastic surgeon's office. This was a year ago, when Ruby The Crazy Corgi accidentally bit off the top of my finger and they had to do a skin graft. If you want to know the full story, you have to read *Why My Third Husband Will Be a Dog,* and it's worth it for the bralessness alone.

But anyway, while I was at the plastic surgeon's, I saw a sign for exfoliating facials, chemical peels, and facial waxing, which made me feel a little better, as I must not be the only woman turning into a man against his/her will.

So I went to the desk to ask the young woman about it, and

it turned out she was an esthetician, which is evidently not someone who appreciates art.

"See my muttonchops?" I asked, pointing. "Can you do anything about that?"

"Not really. It happens as you get older."

Thanks, child. "Can't you wax it off?"

"No."

"But the sign says facial waxing."

"Some women get their mustaches waxed."

I blinked. "So why can't you wax my beard and sideburns?"

The esthetician blinked back. "I don't know. But we don't."

"Don't other women ask for it?"

"Never," she answered without hesitation, which confirmed that I was the only one.

"You got any other ideas?"

"I suppose we could bleach it for you, if you wanted."

"But it's already blond."

"It could be lighter."

"Like Santa Claus or Sigmund Freud?"

"Who?" she asked, but I let it go.

I went home and started plucking like crazy, then yanking and tearing out at the root. But in time, I stopped freaking out and got used to my hairy new self.

I think of my beard as a sweater for the face.

When I have to go out, I pluck my cheeks. No big deal.

And now that it's turning gray, I suppose I'll deal with that, too.

Like a mature adult.

I'll go into denial.

Baby Blues

Daughter Francesca has moved to New York, and it's a matter of public record that I'm officially fine.

Actually, the fact that it's New York is beside the point. For me, the trouble is she's not under my roof anymore.

Or in a convent.

Truth to tell, the only convent I've ever been in was to research my first novel, when I visited a cloistered order of nuns who kept strict vows of silence. Imagine a group of women, living without uttering a single word, 24-7.

Like the worst pajama party ever.

The nuns made an exception to talk to me for my novel, which is proof of heaven, and they told me that silence was the way to the soul and that an empty can makes the most noise.

But to stay on point, Francesca has moved out for good, which I know is the right thing.

For her.

We packed up her books and sweaters, and gradually I watched her bedroom empty until all that was left were some drama-club trophies, a stable of plastic Breyer ponies, and an *I Love Lucy* pillow.

Things she's too old to take, but too young to throw away.

They'll stay and wait for her, holding her place in a time that's becoming history, and a home where she'll no longer feel at home.

She's making a new home.

I gave her my old Pyrex casseroles to take to her apartment, and we poached a tall Oriental lamp from the dining room. I made her take an ergonomic desk chair that she doesn't even like, and I surrendered a painted stool she'll use as a night table. When I look around now, my own house has disintegrated, in a sense, to form hers.

Did my house give birth to her apartment?

And since I don't have to make meals, take time to chat, and generally live with her, the very structure of my days has dematerialized, and I almost feel myself fall to pieces, splintering in a strange sort of way.

It's an odd feeling, though the pieces are slowly coming back together, reconstituted and reconfigured, to form a new life.

After.

Different from Before.

I'm not sure what After will look like, going forward. It won't look like when she was at college, because that was only temporary, a four-year baby step to walking. But now she's flying, and this is something else. Something new. And as happy as I am for her, I'm betting that many of you have felt the same way I do, you mothers and fathers who have happily completed your God-given task of willing a child into and out of your life.

And all of it within memory.

It's a paradox that you can remember your child's first word from twenty years ago and you cannot remember your car keys from twenty minutes ago.

BFFs.

Francesca's first word was "duck," because she had a toy rubber duck. I was fascinated by her first word, and have been fascinated by all of her words since, even the angry and the exasperated words, because there have been so many more joyful, clever, thoughtful, and loving words.

She's a congenitally noisy can, my daughter, and I'm grateful for that. I know that the house will be silent without her, but I also know that we'll probably be on the phone way too much, and that we'll text, email, and even trade paragraphs from whatever we're both writing.

In the end, we'll always have each other's words.

And each other's hearts.

Because, with apologies to my cloistered sisters, I think that voice, and not silence, is the sound of the human soul.

Reading Is Fundamental

Mother Mary has a new job that benefits us all.

Before I reveal it, let me explain that over the years I've made a few author friends, and I buy their books and get them to sign them to my mother, which gives her a big charge. Last month I shipped her five books, including my newest one, then I called to ask her, "How'd you like my book?"

"I loved it, it was great! But I have some corrections for it. And for the others."

"Corrections? How many?"

"About five."

"Five corrections?" I ask, surprised. "Like typos? That's bad."

"No, five pages of corrections. And for the others, too."

I am astounded. "Five pages of typos?"

"Not typos, corrections, and I have five pages per book. So, twenty-five pages of corrections."

Now, I officially don't get it. "Give me an example of something you corrected."

"Okay, in your book, you use the word 'ain't.' 'Ain't' is not a word."

"Is it used in dialogue?"

"Yes."

"Then, it's fine. That's how the character speaks. That's not a mistake."

"Yes, it is. Nobody should use the word 'ain't.' You know better than that, you went to college. I'll mail you the sheets. You'll see."

"Okay, send them."

"'Ain't!' Hmph!"

So Mother Mary mails me the alleged corrections, twenty-five pages of notebook paper, each line written in capitals in a shaky red flair. AIN'T IS NOT A WORD! is the most frequent "correction." A few are typos, but the rest are editorial changes, different word choices, or new endings to the plot.

Bottom line, Mother Mary is a book critic, in LARGE PRINT.

Still, I read the sheets, touched. It must have taken her hours to make the lists, and it's really sweet. I call to tell her so, which is when she lowers the boom:

"You need to send the lists to your friends," she says. "Your friends who wrote the other books. They should know about the mistakes, so they can fix them."

"Okay, Ma, you're right. Thanks. I will."

I don't like lying to my mother, but I'm getting used to it. I figure I'll put the sheets in my jewelry box, with daughter Francesca's letters to Santa Claus. Those corrections are going to the North Pole.

Then my mother adds, "You don't have to worry about the one set, though."

"What one set?"

"A set of corrections, for your new friend." She names a Famous Author who isn't really my new friend, but Somebody

I Wish Were My New Friend. I can't name her here, as she will never be my new friend, now. In fact, she's probably my new enemy. Because my mother sent her five pages of unsolicited editorial changes to her terrific, number-one bestseller.

"You did what?" I ask, faint. "Where did you get her address?"

"Your brother got it from the computer."

"Her address is on the computer?"

"She has an office."

Of course she does. "And you sent it to her?"

"Sure. To help her."

I try to recover. I have only one hope. "You didn't tell her who you are, did you?"

"What do you mean?"

I want to shoot myself for never changing my last name. My last name is Scottoline and so is Mother Mary's, and the Very Famous Author signed a book to her at my request, so in other words . . .

"Oh, sure, I told her I'm your mother, in case she didn't know."

"Great." I sink into a chair. "And you did that because . . ."

"Because I'm proud of you."

Ouch. I can't help but smile. How can I be angry? I tell her, "I'm proud of you, too, Ma."

It's not even a lie.

Begrudging

~~~~~~~~

I'm not one to hold a grudge.

On the contrary.

I don't merely hold a grudge, I wave my grudge proudly. I hoist it like the Statue of Liberty with her torch. I love grudges.

I put the grrrr in grudge.

I have lots of grudges, maybe three hundred of them, and they're always with me, like a Snuggie of bad feelings. And when I travel, I pack my grudges in a roller bag and drag them behind me.

They don't fit in the overhead.

They barely fit in a 727.

But I'm starting to wonder if this is a good thing.

Our story begins with my oldest grudge.

Over twenty years ago, I decided to try to become a writer. I did this to stay home with baby daughter Francesca, but that's not the point. The point is I always wanted to write a novel, and the more I thought about it, the more I wanted to give it a shot. So finally I did, and there followed five years of rejection. My favorite rejection letter came from a New York agent who wrote, "We don't have time to take on any more clients, and if we did, we wouldn't take you."

Ouch.

I've had a grudge against that meanie for almost two decades, and it's one of my favorite grudges.

I'm hoping you can relate. I'm betting somebody done you wrong, at one point. Maybe more than one person. And maybe, like me, you keep mental score, so you can keep hate alive.

If you are a grudge professional, you keep a You-Know-What List. I myself have a You-Know-What Book, Volumes 1–12.

What doesn't kill you makes you bitter.

So here's what happened:

I was signed up to go to Book Expo America, which is a big publishing trade show in New York, and I knew that the aforementioned meanie would be there, because he always goes. Every year, when I spot him, my head explodes and I think felonious thoughts, but I never say anything because he's always across the room or surrounded by people.

Also, I chicken out.

And it's been bothering me for years that I chicken out.

In fact, between being angry at the meanie for the original grudge and being angry at myself for chickening out, I'm packing a lot of bad vibes lately, far too many to carry on the plane.

And now the airlines are charging for checked bags, which also makes me angry. In fact, I'm starting a grudge against the airlines.

So I told my assistant Laura that I would be seeing the meanie, and I asked her how I should handle it. I told her I had three choices: I could tell him he was a jerk to me, or beat him senseless with my latest hardcover, or strangle him with those Spanx I bought and never wore.

You know which answer I preferred.

One size kills all.

And Laura answered, "Don't be bitter, be better."

"Huh wha?" says I.

"You heard me. Be better, not bitter. You're better than that."

"I am?" I asked, but Laura had already hung up.

So I went to the trade show, and sure enough, I saw the object of my disaffection across the room, talking to people. And I promised myself I would not chicken out, yet another year.

Was I bitter or better?

Only one way to find out.

I found myself walking toward him, happy that I had a purse so heavy it could qualify as a lethal weapon.

In case I was accidentally bitter.

I zeroed in on him, and when I got closer, I could see that he was much older than I remembered, or maybe I had never gotten this close to him. When he looked over at me, his pale blue eyes were hooded, and one had a gray rim, like a storm-cloud edging in. His posture was stooped, and his suit hung on him. Still, he smiled at me in a formal way, and I found myself extending my hand to shake his, which felt cool and frail, his knuckles knobby from arthritis.

I introduced myself and asked, "How are you?"

"Fine," he answered, then turned away and went back to his conversation.

He hadn't gotten nicer, he'd just gotten older. And God willing, he was going to die before me.

Suddenly, I felt better. Lighter. Happier. I went outside and called Laura.

"Good for you!" she said. "So you forgave him."

"Are you kidding? I'm better, not crazy," I told her.

And I'm still mad at the airlines.

How To Talk To Moms

By Francesca Scottoline Serritella

Did you hear about the ten-year-old who writes self-help books? His name is Alec Greven, and he penned, or crayon-ed, *How to Talk to Moms*. Presumably, the intended audience is other ten-year-olds, but I think this book could have broader appeal.

Namely, me.

I wasn't attracted to it in some condescending, look-how-cute way either. I need this book. I need help figuring out How To Talk To Mom.

But here's the problem. I need the twenty-four-year-old-just-moved-out version.

As you know, my mom and I are very close. When it comes to the big issues, feelings, emotions, etc., I can always speak frankly with Mom. It's the small stuff I'm sweating.

For instance, last night, I went to see my cousin in Long Island City. No big deal. So I mentioned this mundane outing matter-of-factly to my mother over the phone. But as a matter of fact, she didn't find it so mundane.

"How are you getting there? The subway? At night? ALONE?"

I thought I said, "I am going to see Paul's new apartment," but in Mom-speak that translates to: "I am going to meet certain death in the New York City subway tunnels that are soon to be my tomb."

Talk about lost in translation.

So how should I have said this to avoid throwing Mom into an unrecoverable tailspin of fear and worry?

Recently, I met a nice guy while out at a bar with friends. He's a young lawyer and it turns out he grew up near me and we have a lot in common. I gave him my number and lo and behold, he actually called me to go out. I share this good news with Mom, but again, in plain English. Her response?

"Dinner with a stranger? Did you verify what he told you? He could be anyone, you have no way of knowing."

See, my story in Mom-ese translated to: "I met a guy named Ted Bundy, and I think he really likes me!"

To appease her, I had to Google the guy, find his last five addresses, proof of his alleged alma mater, and one official Notice of Appearance in court to prove he was a practicing (she immediately assumed he was laid-off) lawyer. And she still wanted me to spring for the $19.95 criminal-background check.

I didn't.

God help me the night I actually went on the date.

I understand playing it safe, so my mother and I discussed some strategies on how to protect myself *just in case*. Meet him at the restaurant instead of my apartment, make sure I get in the cab to go home alone, tell my roommate where I'm going and plan when she should call me and expect me back, etc. I thought I had said all the right things in my pre-date Talk With Mom. But I made one critical error, this time, not with what I said, but with what I did NOT say.

I did not say, "I'll call you when I'm home."

Big mistake.

Like, huge.

You see, New York dinners start kind of late, so I was still out at 11:00 p.m. when she texted the first time. And the bar we went to afterwards was loud, so I didn't hear my phone ring at 11:37 p.m. or again around midnight. And we happened to have a conversation about how people who constantly check their BlackBerrys are so annoying, so I kept it in my purse while the four other text messages chimed in. And at the very end of the date, the guy actually seemed to want to kiss me, so when I finally did hear my ringer go off, I quickly silenced it and leaned in.

Kiss of death.

In the cab I saw I had five new text messages, three missed

This is what you get for scaring me.

calls, and two new voicemails. I winced when I listened to the first voicemail and heard my mom's barely controlled voice saying, "Hi, honey. Just making sure you're okay. Please call me when you get home."

But this time, I could translate.

"CALL ME NOW I AM FREAKING OUT!"

I felt terrible. Sure, my mom was overreacting a little (I found out when I did call her that she had even emailed my roommate). But the fact remained that for a couple hours there, she was really scared for me, and all because of a simple breakdown of communication.

So how does the newly moved-out twentysomething talk to Mom?

Alec Greven can't grow up fast enough.

Miles To Go

~~~~~~~

I know I'm supposed to become my mother, but I'm actually becoming my late father.

At least I thought of him recently, when I checked the mileage on my car. I'm at 94,272, and I've watched it inch up from 94,109 and before that, 93,820. I check my mileage more often than I check my weight, and that's saying something. On a long trip, I watch my mileage like it's a movie with Brad Pitt.

I can't get enough.

Bottom line, I'm way too involved with my car mileage. The more miles I have, the happier I get. I dream about hitting 100,000 miles like some people dream about hitting the lottery.

Why?

It makes me feel as if I've accomplished something, though I haven't. It's my car that's done all the work. I'm just along for the ride. Still, every time I hit a new 10,000-mile mark, I feel like celebrating.

Growing up, I remember The Flying Scottolines driving around in our '64 Corvair Monza, and my father pointing to the mileage counter as the little white numbers turned slowly to something. He was so excited that we all clapped, but I didn't understand why.

Now I'm excited, and I still don't understand why.

I used to think it was because if I accumulated enough miles, I could justify getting a new car. But that's not it. I love my car and want to be buried in it, with a Diet Coke in the cupholder.

At around 17,328,000,000 miles.

But I'm wondering if my mileage thing is related to my Things To Do list thing. I love having a Things To Do list, and over the years, I perfected a template for my Things To Do list. I write the list of Things To Do on the right, and on the left, next to each Thing, I draw a big circle. I get to check the circle only after each Thing is Done.

Oh boy, I love checking those circles.

I make a big check, like a schoolteacher at the top of your homework. Then I stand before my list and survey with satisfaction all the checked circles.

And oddly, I admit that I've added to the list a Thing I've Already Done, just so I can check the circle.

I know, right?

It's kind of kooky.

So I told this to a friend of mine, and she told me she does things this kooky, and she also added another kooky thing. She has an electronic reader, and at the bottom of each page, it tells you what percentage of the book you've read. As you read the book, the percentage increases, and she has found herself watching the percentage increase as she reads. She's gotten used to the fact that she read 57% of a book, as opposed to 45 chapters, and she's even figured out how many pages it takes to increase the percentage a point. The other night, she couldn't go to sleep because she had read 96% of the book and she had to get to 100%.

Okay, the friend is me.

I'm sensing that these three things—mileage counters, Things To Do, and reading percentages—are related.

Am I taking a task-oriented approach to life?

Or am I celebrating the small things?

Or both?

There's a great quote by E. L. Doctorow, who says, "Writing is like driving at night in the fog. You can only see as far as your headlights, but you can make the whole trip that way."

I sense this quote is related, too, and that it applies not only to writing, but to everything, at least for me. Because writing a novel is like driving to Toronto or cleaning your house or starting *War and Peace*. Any large task is intimidating at the beginning, but it's doable if it's broken down, mile by mile, Thing by Thing, percentage point by percentage point. And when you finally finish that task, you can check the circle.

Have a Diet Coke, for me.

And my father.

One Down

Mother Mary never forgets anything. Take the Case of the Crossword-Puzzle Cookie Jar.

Our story begins when I see an ad for a cookie jar in the newspaper. It's a square white jar with a real crossword puzzle on each of the four sides, and it has a special pen that you use to fill in the blanks. Plus it comes with heart-shaped cookies that I don't have to bake myself.

Mother Mary loves crossword puzzles, though she doesn't much care for cookies, regardless of shape. Bottom line, the crossword-puzzle cookie jar struck me as a great gift for Mother's Day. At the time I saw the ad, it was a month in advance of the holiday, so I ordered it online, charged it to my credit card, and specified that it be sent to her. Then I ordered her flowers like I always do and figured I had Mother's Day squared away.

But when I called her for Mother Mary's Day, she'd gotten the flowers but not the crossword-puzzle cookie jar. It never came. She was happy with her flowers and didn't mind not getting the jar. She told me to make sure I wasn't charged for it. I wasn't worried. I assumed they hadn't charged me, because something had clearly gone wrong. The next week, she called me.

She said, "I saw an ad for that cookie jar, and that thing cost a hundred bucks."

"I know."

"That's too much to spend on me."

"No, it's not," I say, because I'm such a sport. I'm the kind of daughter who promises her mother gifts that never arrive. And cookies that other people bake.

"Did you check and see if they charged you?"

"The statement didn't come in yet, but I will."

"Make sure you do. Mark my words."

Then, every time I call to say hi, the first thing she asks is:

"Did you make sure they didn't charge you for that cocka-mamie cookie jar?"

"Not yet. Don't you want it? I can call and ask them to send you another one."

"No, I don't want it. It costs too much. I just want to make sure they don't charge you."

"They won't."

"How do you know? Don't be a patsy."

I smile. *Patsy* is a great word. More people should use it. "Okay, I'll check."

I hang up, vowing to check my credit-card statement when it comes in. The next week, she calls me.

"I slept terrible last night," she says.

"Why?"

"This thing with that cookie jar. It's keeping me up."

"Why?"

"It's a scam."

I blink. "What?"

"Lots of people like crossword puzzles, right?"

"Right."

"And lots of people like cookies."

"Except you."

"Right. So. The company says they'll send the cookie jars, but they don't, and nobody checks to see if they got charged, and the next thing you know, they're off on a cruise."

"Financed by cookie jars?"

"You got it!"

I hang up, this time vowing I will never order her anything from the newspaper, or anywhere else. Every gift I will buy and carry to her, or else she'll have a heart attack for Mother's Day.

But last week the statement finally came in, and I checked it.

You know what?

They charged me.

But I'm not telling.

The Right To Choose

~~~~~~

Let's talk about a decision that women have to make every morning:

Big purse or little purse?

I know it's not life or death, but it makes you nuts if you choose the wrong one as consistently as I do.

If you carry a big purse for the day, it's guaranteed that you'll end up never needing anything you're lugging around like a pack animal. And if you carry a little purse for the day, you'll invariably end up tucking things under your armpit or asking your husband to carry them.

It's Purse Lotto, and there are winners and losers, every day.

I lose, almost always. I keep track, and if I choose the right purse four days out of seven, I'm Purse Diva. Most weeks, I choose correctly only one day.

Purse Geek.

Now I can already hear you menfolk, thinking that the problem can be solved by a medium-size purse. That seems sensible, but it doesn't work.

Not your fault, gentlemen. How would you know? Unless you carry a man purse, in which case, play along.

In reality, a medium purse is the worst of both worlds. It's not big enough to carry everything you need, and it's not small enough to let you feel footloose and fancy-free. And besides, medium defeats the purpose of adding fun to your life by gambling with handbags.

So I say, live dangerously. Choose big or little. Pick your poison. See if, by the end of the day, you're a Purse Hero or a Purse Loser.

Use me as your inspiration. You couldn't do worse.

Just the other day, I chose a big purse and ended up walking all over NYC with Daughter Francesca, carrying the weight of the world on my shoulder. I didn't need the hardback book, full makeup case, or water bottle.

Turns out they have water in New York, too.

So the next day, I carried a cute little purse, but wrong again. I couldn't zip it up after I bought a pack of gum, so I walked everywhere worried that my keys would fall out or I'd get pick-pocketed. And Francesca had to carry our umbrella, newspaper, and everything else in her nice big purse.

It goes without saying that the day you choose the wrong purse, your daughter will choose the right one. Last week, Francesca was six for seven.

Purse Diva.

It was the same week I got so frustrated that I opted out of Purse Lotto altogether. Francesca and I went to a movie, and I carried only my wallet.

Whoa. I threw caution to the summer wind. I went free and easy, like July itself.

Francesca looked over. "Why no purse?"

"Traveling light."

"You should carry a purse, Mom."

"Don't need one."

We settled into our seats at the movie, and Francesca gestured at my wallet. "Where are you gonna put that?"

I blinked. The seat to the right of me was taken, and my cupholder held a Diet Coke and Raisinets. I couldn't admit defeat and ask her to put my wallet in her big purse, so I set the wallet under my chair, on the sticky floor. Yuck.

"See?" I said, hiding my distaste. "No problem."

It worked out perfectly until we left the theater, got several blocks away, and I remembered that my wallet was still on the floor. We hurried back, and it was still there, probably because even felons couldn't unstick it. Then we went out to dinner.

"Now where are you gonna put the wallet?" Francesca asked, lifting an eyebrow.

"Right here." I set it down on the empty chair next to me, no problem. I didn't forget it either. But when we had gotten a few blocks from the restaurant, I realized that I'd been so worried about my wallet, I'd left my credit card on the table. We hurried back, for the second time that day.

So now I lose at Wallet Lotto, too.

"I shoulda brought a purse," I said, going home, after all was recovered.

"Next time." Francesca patted me on the back. "Don't feel bad."

"Which purse should I have brought, oh sage one?"

"The small."

Purse Genius.

Braless in the ER, The Sequel

So the other night, right before bed, I was standing with my dogs in the backyard, and here's what happened to me:

A bug flew in my ear.

You heard that right.

But I didn't.

I heard nothing but a loud and freaky fluttering.

Do you follow? I don't mean that a bug landed on my ear and flew away, which would hardly be worth whining about. What I mean is that a bug flew into my ear and got stuck inside my head.

Can I just say that I freaked out?

I ran around the yard, yelling and shaking my head so hard that my new glasses flew off and broke.

Great.

I slapped my ear with my hand, but the bug just kept fluttering, giving me the creepiest case of swimmer's ear ever. I figured it was a moth because it sounded like it had big wings, and it tickled, not in a good way. I shivered, I shuddered, I was grossed out. I couldn't stand still. Nor could I deal with the fact that there was a moth inside my head.

I tried to remember from Biology 101 if the moth could fly

into my brain, but I was pretty sure that it had to stop at my eardrum, which was already starting to itch, hurt, and maybe even vibrate.

Okay, that could have been my imagination.

Because there was a *moth inside my head*!

I didn't know what to do. I considered sucking it out with the vacuum cleaner, but I don't have the kind with the hose, only the kind you roll on the floor. I thought about pouring water into my ear but then I'd end up with a soggy moth. I tried to pull it out but it was already too far in, and I was worried I'd push it in even farther, maybe to my cerebellum or eyes.

I didn't do well in Biology 101.

Then it seemed like the moth was going farther inside my noggin. Hitting myself in the temple wasn't doing anything but giving me a headache. I tried to stay calm but every time the moth pounded its wings, it sounded like a helicopter.

Okay, maybe that's an exaggeration.

But still, it was scary, like that horror movie where the fly crawls up the girl's nose. I tried to decide whether I'd rather have a fly up my nose or a moth in my ear, but I was too panicky to think. I ran back inside the house and danced around, yelping and trying to knock the moth out.

The dogs watched with varying reactions. The goldens sat calmly, waiting to go upstairs to bed, but Little Tony and Ruby The Corgi started barking and running around, a canine version of me. Also I was dog-sitting Pip, Daughter Francesca's spaniel, and though he remained quiet, his bored expression told me he wished he'd stayed at a hotel.

So I drove at breakneck speed to the emergency room, and thank God there was almost no one on the road because the moth went into winged overdrive, and I yelped and squirmed the entire way. I explained everything to the nice reception ladies at the hospital, who told me that this happened all the time and were kind enough to understand my need to keep moving. It was the people in the waiting room who raised an eyebrow, thinking I was having seizures. And I didn't take offense when one of the nurses asked if I had taken any street drugs.

By the way, for those of you who recall my last trip to the emergency room, after my dog bit the hand that feeds her, I had yet another superhot male nurse. And yes, I was braless while middle-aged.

Which would be the bad news.

The good news is that while they took my blood pressure, the moth flew out of my ear. One nurse gasped, the other one laughed.

At least the moth didn't fly out my other ear.

And you know what? I killed the moth.

I felt instantly guilty, but he deserved it.

Then I went home, once again, happily empty-headed.

The next day the receptionist called to tell me I had left my driver's license and insurance card at the hospital, and she asked me whether I'd write a story about the moth.

Ya think?

Five Dog Night

We know that I live alone with five dogs, which sounds pathetic, but is actually fun.

We also know that I sleep with at least four of these dogs. The two Cavaliers, Little Tony and Peach His Child Bride, then Penny and Ruby The Corgi with Restless Leg Syndrome.

Angie, the older golden, sleeps in my bedroom on her denim dog bed that says GOOD GIRLS.

All the bad girls are in my bed.

Now this is going to sound weird, but I actually look forward to going to bed, partly because of these canine characters.

Here's a typical night: I usually work until bedtime in the family room, while the dogs doze, chew Nylabones, or watch TV. It's not always as peaceful as it sounds. Ruby barks every time a doorbell rings in a commercial, and she hates the one where the people drive around squeezing a squeaky toy. Somebody needs to tell these advertisers not to make commercials that make dogs bark. I mute the commercial every time it comes on, and if I ever see whatever product they're selling, I'll burn it.

Anyway, my favorite part of the day is when I turn off the laptop and TV, switch off the table lamps, and walk the dogs one last time. It takes a while for five dogs to go to the bathroom, and I use that time to look up at the sky and the stars. I'm not good at constellations, but I recognize the three little stars in a row as part of Orion. I know a belt when I see one. I'm good at stellar accessories.

If they had constellations in the shape of shoes and handbags, I'd be an astronomer.

In fact, it makes you wonder if there are enough women astronomers. I have a feeling that if there were, we'd see fewer dippers and bears in the sky and more eyelash curlers and mascara wands.

I would never be outside on a freezing night if it weren't for these doggies, and believe it or not, that's fun, too. The air is pure and clean, and it's easy to forget how cold it is if you're bundled up. The sky in winter is the color of frozen blueberries, and last night was almost starless except for a full moon, so bright that when it shone through the bare tree limbs, it cast jagged moonshadows on the frozen ground, like lightning.

I like to look up at the sky because my only other choice is looking down, at what the dogs are doing. And it doesn't get more earthbound.

When they're finished, we go in, lock up, and trundle upstairs, where everybody falls into position. Penny and Ruby take opposite corners, anchoring the bed, and Peach and Little Tony take their places on my left and right, anchoring me.

Peach cuddles like crazy, curling in the crook of my elbow or against my neck. They say Cavaliers are lap dogs, but that's not true. They're really neck dogs. Face dogs. Cheek dogs. They want to breathe the same air as you, at the exact same moment, like the stalkers of the dog world.

And you know what?

It's kinda great.

And Peach, especially, is so calm. She never yaps or growls, and is somehow the one who keeps her head when all the dogs around her are losing theirs.

Which has been known to happen at night.

Anybody who sleeps with dogs knows that they bark at squirrels, deer, and whatever else is out there. Or they start scratching and shake the bed. Or they shift positions and squirm around. Or they have doggie dreams that make them yelp. Or they decide to clean themselves, and the sound of their licking will wake you up, then gross you out.

If you sleep with dogs, it won't be the best night's sleep.

But somehow, it won't matter.

Bizarro Birthdays

~~~~~~~~

I just got off the phone with Mother Mary, who's lost her mind. Or maybe it's Scottoline birthday madness.

Let me explain.

She told me a story that happened to her that day, when she was going outside to do the laundry.

Yes, you read that right.

She lives in Miami with brother Frank and she goes outside to do the laundry because they keep their washer and dryer in the backyard.

This makes no sense to me, but she swears that it's common in Florida to keep major appliances in the backyard, like shrubs with twenty-year warranties.

Still, it's hard for me to believe. I suspect that my mother and brother are redneck Italians.

But never mind, that's not the point of the story.

So Mother Mary is going outside to put in a load of laundry and she sees one of her neighbors, a nice young woman, walking her two-year-old son by the hand. My mother stops to say hello, and the little boy looks up at her with big blue eyes and says:

"I love you, Mary."

So of course my mother melts, because she loves kids, and she even gets choked up telling me on the phone. The whole story is sounding really sweet until she gets to the next part, which is when she asks the mother of the toddler when is his birthday, and the woman answers:

November 23.

Okay, means nothing to you, but that's brother Frank's birthday.

And on the phone, my mother tells me: "I looked at that little boy, and I thought he was like Frank. Like he has your brother's soul."

I thought I heard her wrong. "Pardon?"

"When he said he loved me, I looked into his eyes and I could see his soul, and it was Frank's soul."

"You mean they're alike?"

"No, I mean they're the same."

I tried to deal. "You're kidding, right?"

"No. I'm telling you, he has the same exact blue eyes as Frank and he was born on the same day. He has Frank's soul."

"Ma, Frank still has his soul. He's not dead yet."

"I know that," she said, irritably. "They share the same soul."

"Ma, that's crazy."

"Sorry, but I know, I can tell. Remember the earthquake?"

This shuts me up, temporarily. It's matter of public record that Mother Mary was the only person in Miami to feel an earthquake that took place in Tampa, and the South Florida newspapers even dubbed her Earthquake Mary. Ever since then, she thinks she's Al Roker, but supernatural.

She said, "It's the same soul. Absolutely."

"Ma, just because they have the same birthday doesn't mean they have the same soul."

"Hmph. What do you know about birthdays?"

She was referring to something I'll never live down, which happened to me over twenty years ago, when Daughter Francesca was three years old. I had taken her in a stroller into an optician's shop in town, and a man walked through the door, pointed directly at Francesca, and said: "Her birthday is February 6."

I was astounded. "How do you know?"

"I just do."

I went home that day and called my mother. "Ma, some guy just guessed that Francesca's birthday is February 6! Isn't that amazing?"

"No."

"Why not?"

"Because her birthday is February 7."

I blinked. "It is?"

"Yes, dummy."

Look, I have no idea how it happened, but for the first three years of Francesca's life, I celebrated her birthday on the wrong day.

Sue me.

Maybe it's because I was in labor for 349,484 hours, so the exact day she was born seemed like a technicality. And since then, it was just she and I celebrating a day earlier, with nobody around to know better.

So now I can never say anything about birthdays, ever.

But at least I know where everybody's soul should be.

And their washer-dryers, too.

Focused

~~~~~~~~

I'm trying to understand why I have six different pairs of eyeglasses. I'm only one woman, with two nearsighted eyes.

I realized this odd state of affairs when I decided that I would finally replace my glasses, which were crooked because I had put them on the bedside table one night and didn't reach far enough, so they fell to the floor. I was too tired to pick them up and figured I'd get them in the morning, which I did.

With my foot.

I specialize in ruining glasses. I sit on them, drop them face-down, set thick books on them, and put them in the case wrong, snapping off a stem. Freud would say I don't like wearing glasses.

Guy's a genius.

Anyway I wore my broken glasses for a week, but I got tired of looking drunk, so I bought a new pair. We won't talk about how much they cost, because now you need a second mortgage to buy glasses, which is why I never throw any away, but that's not my point.

My point is that now I own a new pair of normal glasses, a pair of ancient prescription sunglasses I use for the beach and yard work, a pair of semi-ancient prescription sunglasses I use

for driving and everything else, a pair of non-prescription sunglasses, and a pair of wacky zany kooky reading glasses, which
is either the mark of a true eccentric or a middle-aged woman.

Or both.

My wacky zany kooky readers look like spin art on the board-
walk, in fuchsia and turquoise with weird swirls of gold. I've
found that even the most conservative woman will wear wacky
zany kooky readers. In fact, the more conservative the woman,
the wackier the readers. Secretly, I think we're all sending the
same message, which is:

I'm not dead yet.

I'm letting my freak flag fly.

Also you're not the boss of me.

Yay, us!

Anyway, to stay on point, how can I have so many glasses?
Every time I go anywhere, my purse is full of glasses cases. And
the craziest part?

I also have contacts.

I got contacts in the sixth grade, after somebody told me,
"Men don't make passes at girls who wear glasses."

Ouch.

Back then, contact lenses were made of actual glass, so you
had to get used to them by wearing them for a month, blinking and tearing, in continuous eye pain. I never really got used
to them, so you could tell I was wearing contacts by the ten-
tative backward tilt to my head as I walked, like someone
crossing a rickety rope bridge in the Amazon.

Plus the glass contacts were always popping out of my eyes,
and everybody in the vicinity would end up on all fours, picking through the rug. The only good part was that I learned to

shoot them out of my eyes for fun, by pressing down on the side of the lens, playing corneal tiddlywinks.

Sorry, only people old enough to remember glass contacts will get the tiddlywinks reference. All others, please humor me.

Anyway, it was a lot of trouble to go through for men to make passes, and then Thing One and Thing Two happened, so what does that tell you?

But now it turns out that contacts and glasses aren't good enough, because there's a new goop that women can put on their eyelids if they have "inadequate lashes."

Wha?

The ads say, "It's your own eyelashes—only better."

Thank God my eyelashes can be better. I had no idea they were underachieving. I have slacker eyelashes.

The ad also says you can "grow your own lashes!"

This is a novel idea. I grow my own tomatoes. I grow my own basil. I never thought of growing my own body parts, for limbs and appendages that weren't up to snuff.

Given my druthers, I'd bypass the lashes and grow more boobs.

I bet men would make passes at me, then. Even if I wore glasses.

I smell Thing Three.

But if you ask me, this eye business has gotten out of hand.

First glasses weren't good enough, so I got contacts. Now my eyes aren't good enough.

So will I buy this eyelash goop?

No. I'm older and wiser, and I draw the line.

And I don't mean eyeliner.

Fool me once, shame on me. Fool me twice?

Okay, that happens.

But three times?

Never.

I have plenty of glasses, contacts, and eyelashes, thank you.

I can see clearly now.

My vision is, finally, perfect.

Breezy

The great thing about summer is that we all take the time to slow down, which is especially necessary in a world buzzing with laptops and BlackBerrys. Today I am marveling at the most perfect low-tech invention of all time:

The fan.

How great is a fan? No bells, whistles, or BTUs. It's plastic, and it costs only fifteen dollars. You can't even buy gum for fifteen dollars. I am in love with my fan, even though I have bad childhood memories of same.

Let me back up.

Growing up, we had no air-conditioning, and I remember going to my friends' houses, where they did. My best friend Rachel had something mysterious and great called Central Air, and we loved it so much that we would leave her house only for the movies, where they had air-conditioning and a blue banner that advertised as much, in letters so cold that they formed icicles.

Remember that sign?

Please say yes.

Anyway at home, we had window fans, which were the source of much discord. The big debate was whether to turn them out or in. To me, even at age twelve, this was a no-brainer. One side blows air at you, and one side doesn't. So which side should face you, as you sweat your butt off?

Of course.

Stick the fan in the window, so that it blows air on you. My father, brother, and I were aligned on this opinion, but we did not prevail, as we lived with a meteorologist.

Mother Mary.

You may not have known she was a meteorologist, but she was, when it came to interior weather. By the way, she was also a doctor, when it came to swimming after eating. And an electrician, when it came to toasters near water. Mothers are women of invisible degrees, and she was no exception.

Mother Mary held that the fan should be in the window turned out, so that it did not blow on you. Her theory was that if it was turned out, it would suck all the hot air from the room and blow it outside, thus cooling the room. Sadly, the fan came with no instructions to settle the argument, and in the end, you know who prevailed, so we turned our window fans out and sweated in our living room.

Yes, it sucked.

Mother Mary also believed in cross-ventilation. In fact, if you ever meet her, don't get her started on cross-ventilation. She can talk about cross-ventilation like some people talk about politics. According to her, you should throw open two windows opposite from each other, and the air from one window will be sucked in, whoosh magically across the room, and blow out the other window, thus cooling all the Scottolines sweating inside.

This sucked, too.

We waited and waited for a breeze to cross-ventilate us, yet it never happened. So we whined and whined for an air conditioner, and one day, they relented, albeit with a compromise. We would use fans and cross-ventilation in the living room, and in the dining room, we installed a window air conditioner, which supposedly had enough BTUs to cool the entire first floor.

It didn't.

It cooled the dining room, but we never used the dining room except for Christmas, Easter, or another day when something really good happened to Jesus Christ.

And the TV was in the living room, so we were always in the living room, sweating amid the inside-out fans and non-existent cross-ventilation, while the dining room remained empty, if frosty.

When I grew up, I got to be the mother, so my house has central air, window air conditioners, and fans.

Overcompensate, much?

But this summer has been so cool that I'm using only the fan. It sits in the window next to my bed and whirrs pleasantly all night, cooling dogs, cats, and one middle-aged woman.

And it blows inside, the way God and General Electric intended.

Be Home By Ten, Mom

~~~~~~

By Francesca Scottoline Serritella

For a little girl, watching her mother get ready for a night out is an education. I remember being mesmerized as my mother would line her eyes to a feline contour, or wrap her curly hair around a round brush and, with a wave of her magic hair-dryer, pull it into straight, spun gold. I would eagerly slip my feet into whichever pairs of heels did not make the cut for that evening's outfit, and by the time I was four, I could lipstick my lips without a smudge.

Today, I can balance in stilettos of my own, and I graduated from regular eyeliner and went on to get my master's in liquid liner.

So when my mom called me last week asking what she should wear on her date that Saturday, I thought, can I possibly teach my mother, the master, anything about getting ready for a date?

Five minutes into the conversation I realized, yes, God yes, I could help my mother. In fact, I must.

Girlfriend wanted to wear a suit on the date. Blazer and all, the same uniform she wears to meet with her editor. "I feel comfortable in that," she said.

Yeah, because a date is the most fun when you treat it like a professional interview. But hey, if he gets to asking about "benefits," you should throw a drink in his face.

No, Mom, you cannot wear a suit.

"But I look dumpy in my jeans." Truth: my mom does not look dumpy. She and I wear the same size jeans. She is a tiny rocket ship that runs on love and worry. But I can't convince her of this, so we compromise on black pants.

"My friend told me men like boots. But I think boots are workin' it too much, right?"

I was immediately reminded of when I was eleven and my best friend told me that boys like it when you drink from a straw at the far corner of your mouth. For years, any visit to the mall food court was a chance for my soda-straw act. I don't know what look I was going for—maybe "sexy dental patient"—or who my target audience was—Dr Pepper?—but it failed.

Trying to be seductive with a cheap plastic straw is workin' it too much.

Anyway, I said, "Boots are fine. You're supposed to work it a little, it's a date!"

"And so a long sweater, maybe that blue one?" She went on to describe a sweater she owns that is the size and shape of a bathrobe. I borrowed it once, but I thought it was a dress.

"With the pants? It's way too long."

"But I have to cover my butt!" According to my mother, a burka would be flattering as long as it was black.

And then, I don't know why I said it, because it's creepy and dorky at the same time, but I said, "Mom, you have to show the wares!"

I actually said *wares*. I know, it was weird.

A few days later, she called me again. "Wanna hear something funny?" She went on to tell me about how her date selected a restaurant that just so happens to be where her ex-husband (not my dad) proposed to her. We laughed at the irony.

"But you didn't mention that to him, right?"

Silence.

"You *did*?"

"It's a funny story!"

I bet he thought it was a laugh riot.

Soon, a neutral location was agreed upon, wardrobe decisions were finalized, and the big day was upon us. Well, upon her.

One supportive daughter.

But I was nervous for her! All day, I worried—what if she resorts to the bathrobe sweater at the last minute? What if she gets something in her teeth and doesn't notice? What if this guy doesn't see how totally adorable she is? What if he hurts her feelings?

Saturday night, I went to a movie with a friend, but the whole night I was checking my phone to see if my mother had called or texted. When she finally called at midnight, I picked up the phone on the first ring.

"How was it?"

"Aw, it didn't go so well."

My heart sank. I was already hatching revenge plots against the cad when she continued, "He was nice, but I'm not sure I'm interested."

I breathed a sigh of relief. Not everyone is lucky enough to hang out with my fashionable, smooth, totally cool mom.

Just me.

Prince Charles

~~~~~~~~

I've decided that refrigerator doors are bulletin boards for moms.

Not like the bulletin boards you remember from school, covered with construction paper cut-outs of hearts on Valentine's Day. Or the bulletin boards at the supermarket, showing phone numbers for hungry painters. I'm talking about that bulletin board you had in middle school. The one that hung in your bedroom. The one that conveyed no information, but was all about things that mattered to you.

Your very identity, under thumbtacks.

I had one, as you can tell.

I still remember it, and it had school photos of my friends, with identical smiles and fake-sky backgrounds. It had my choir pin and a felt letter from the JV tennis team. It had, embarrassingly, a picture of Prince Charles from the cover of *Time* magazine. I always thought he'd make a good husband.

He could have been Thing Three.

Or King Thing Three.

Well, the other day, I went to the refrigerator to get some milk, and something fell off the door. I bent over and picked it up, which was when I realized that it was Daughter Francesca's report card.

From seventh grade.

As you may recall, she's 24 years old.

It made me take a look at my refrigerator door, and I'm betting it's not all that different from yours. Its double doors are completely covered by layers of stuff, with the oldest on the bottom, like the sentimental strata of the earth.

The top layer is all of Francesca's report cards, and they date from middle school to her college graduation. I can't explain why I posted her report cards on the refrigerator when she no longer lived here, but I was so proud of her, even in absentia. Another clue is provided by the other stuff in the top layer, namely, a photo of a mother polar bear and her cub, a photo of a mother horse and her colt, and a photo of a mother elephant and her—

You know where this is going.

The only other stuff in the top layer is birth announcements with baby pictures and Christmas cards with baby pictures. Half of these kids are driving now, but I can't bring myself to take down their pictures.

How can you throw a baby in the trash?

I found most of the top layer in magazines and newspapers, and when I see something dorky but adorable, I clip it out and hang it on the fridge. I have to tape it up because my refrigerator is stainless steel, so by the second layer, even the tape is old. I think of that layer as the hokey layer, which is closely related to the top layer, in terms of emotionality. It contains photos that inspire, like one of a prima ballerina performing a soaring split in mid-air, and another of Olympian Shaun White flying upside-down on a snowboard.

Can you tell I'm afraid of heights?

The third layer is evidently the funny layer, plastered with cartoons.

You want it when?

My favorite cartoon is by Robert Mankoff of *The New Yorker,* and it shows a man on the phone at his desk, with a caption that reads, "No, Thursday's out. How about never—is never good for you?"

God bless Robert Mankoff.

He could be Thing Four.

The other cartoons, all about work deadlines and nasty book critics, make me look more beleaguered than I actually feel. Whoever is doing all this clipping and taping needs to stay away from the refrigerator.

My Sub-Zero suggests that I'm subpar.

The fourth layer is the throwback layer, and part of me is relieved it's so hard to find, underneath the inspirational kittens. There lie photos of The Rolling Stones, Bob Dylan, and a young Michael Jackson.

Also Eleanor Roosevelt, but she didn't have a band.

Finally, the last layer on the refrigerator door contains all manner of diet information, like lists of calories, a chart of South Beach Diet foods, and an index of Weight Watcher points. This layer hasn't been seen in a decade, and I suspect it came with the refrigerator.

I bet all of this stuff can be dated by its layers, like the rings of a tree. In the end, it's one woman's life.

Frozen in time.

How I Spent My Summer Staycation

Mother Mary is visiting, and Daughter Francesca has come down from New York, so three generations of Scottoline women are under the same roof. Some call this a family staycation, but I call it a slow death.

With excellent meatballs.

The problem is that we spend the first few days staying inside and watching only my mother's favorite TV shows, *Law & Order, CSI, NCIS,* and *Cold Case.* Bottom line, she loves anything with a corpse, and I begin to feel like one. Then one night at dinner, a miracle happens.

Wait.

Let me back up.

Most people have a list of Things To Do, but Mother Mary has a list of Things Not To Do. Or more accurately, Things Never To Do. At the top of the list is Don't Go To The Movies. Other entries include Don't Eat Outside With The Bugs and Don't Walk All Over This Cockamamie Mall.

To stay on point, the last movie she went to was *Fantastic Voyage,* which came out in 1966. I'm not making this up. She took Brother Frank and me, and I remember nothing about the movie except Raquel Welch, who wore a cleavage-baring jump-suit that caused my mother to pronounce the movie "dirty."

We up and left.

In any event, since then, I've asked my mother to approxi-mately 3,937,476 movies, but she always says no. Nobody knows why Mother Mary doesn't do the things she doesn't do, and to inquire is to end up in a tautological trap, like a Mobius strip of conversational hell. For example, I did ask her, and the conver-sation went exactly like this:

"Ma, why don't you go to the movies?"

"Because I don't."

"But what's the reason?"

"The reason is, I don't."

"That's not a reason. I want to know the reason."

"Why?"

"I just do."

"Why is that a reason for you, but not for me?"

Honestly, I couldn't reply. I may have a law degree, but my mother is Perry Mason.

In time, I stopped asking about the movies, and it was Daugh-ter Francesca who popped the question, over a meal of over-cooked broccoli, since also on my mother's list is Don't Eat Vegetables That Retain A Hint Of Color.

Francesca said, "Hey, why don't we go see *Julie & Julia*? It's supposed to be good."

Mother Mary answered, "Okay."

I thought I'd heard her wrong. "What?"

My mother looked over. "So?"

We eyed each other warily, but Francesca is no dummy, so

she got up, grabbed a wallet and car keys, and hustled my mother out of the house with the speed of a kidnapper.

In no time, we were sitting at the theater with popcorn, soda, and Raisinets. I kept checking, and Mother Mary was laughing away. She's only four-foot-eleven, so the big seat seemed to swallow her whole and her feet didn't touch the floor. The flickering lights danced across her bifocals, and her white hair was a tiny cloud in the dark theater.

I leaned over. "So, Ma, it turns out that going to the movies is fun, huh?"

My mother looked over. "You couldn't leave it alone, could you?"

I said nothing, because she was absolutely right. I couldn't leave it alone. In fact, I never leave it alone. All of a sudden, at

Three generations of trouble.

Mother Mary naps after her trip to the cockamamie mall.

the movie, I realized that I have my own list of Things Not To Do, and well, you know where this is going.

Then, a day later, we were back at the dinner table over the barely green green beans, and my mother remarked that her cell phone got bad reception. I agreed, and Francesca asked, "So why don't we go to the mall and get a new phone?"

My mother answered, "Okay."

I looked over at my mother, and she looked back at me, playing mother-daughter eye-chicken. We both knew that she never went to the cockamamie mall, but her eyes dared me to leave it alone.

And for once, I did.

Foxy

It's the time of year when nature comes too close for comfort. My spiders are back, which means that when I open the front door, they rush over the threshold, scurry into the living room, and take the good chair.

Now, there's new news.

A grasshopper throws himself against the front door every morning. Each day when I come down, I see him. He jumps up, bonks his head on the door, then lands and looks up, only to try again. I named him Sisyphus and have gone from admiring his persistence to doubting his sanity. I took a picture of him on the threshold, before he jumps. If I look closely, I can see his deranged gleam.

Lately I was wondering if it's the same stubborn grasshopper, or a team of less stubborn grasshoppers, rotating the chore. Either way, he's gone by the afternoon, when I see other grasshoppers in the front yard, who jump and then fly, which is a neat trick. They look like him, so I assume he's one of them, but if I could jump and fly, I wouldn't be wasting my time trying to get inside anybody's house. I'd have a reality TV show.

Anyway, between the spiders and the grasshopper, I stopped using the front door and began using the back door.

Until Little Tony's frog.

Yes, there's a small green frog who hangs out near my back door. He's there every night, and when I open the door, he jumps once, then pretends he's a rock. Jumping and impersonating a rock isn't as cool as jumping and flying, but who am I to judge? I can't do any tricks, except maybe writing a book.

Anyway, when the frog goes into rock mode, he fools my two golden retrievers and Ruby The Corgi. They trot past him, happy to accept that rocks jump only on occasion. But Little Tony, the Cavalier spaniel, knows better.

He sits at the back door all day long, waiting for nightfall. As soon as the frog appears, Little Tony paws at the door, and I let him out, because he wants to be with the frog. He doesn't try to bite or chase it, he just sits next to it, happily.

Bottom line, Little Tony has a pet frog.

Or maybe a pet rock.

I don't want to disturb them, so now I use the back door only during the day, and the rest of the time, I am trapped inside my house by spiders, grasshoppers, and one very clever rock.

Nature finds its way inside, however. It all begins with a fox, crossing my backyard. He's orange and fluffy and appears every day at about five o'clock, then vanishes. Inside the house, his appearance creates havoc. The goldens bark, Ruby The Corgi runs in circles, and Little Tony eats the window. The fox laughs and runs away.

But the fox doesn't come back for about a month, and when he returns, he looks terrible. He's skinny, and his fur is mottled. He scratches his ears constantly. He needs help, so I call all the animal control people, who tell me it's not their problem and suggest I catch him in a Havahart trap. I'm going out to buy one when I find him on the driveway, dead.

The dogs do a victory dance around him, but I feel sad.

Until one night, when I'm trying to sleep and all of them are scratching their ears, their feet thumping against the floor. I turn on the light, wondering. The next day I take the dogs to the vet, and it turns out that they have mange. They get treated, and it will go away in a month.

But not before I notice a rash on my neck, near my ear.

And boy, does it itch.

I call the vet. "What exactly is mange?"

"A type of parasite."

"Can people get mange?"

"I get it all the time," says he.

Yuck. "What do you do for it?"

"Wait it out. They take two weeks to die."

I consider this.

I'm already single enough.

I'm on my way to the doctor, now.

Deadline Fever

The good news is that I didn't have mange. The bad news is that I had poison sumac and a deadline.

Or as I think of it, a dreadline.

To explain, it takes me a year to write a novel, and my deadline just passed, on a Monday. Below is a rewind of the week leading up to the deadline, with play-by-play medical updates. Please tell me you've had weeks like this, because poison sumac loves company.

Our story begins on Monday morning, when my satellite radio stops working. It flashes Acquiring Signal, even though it isn't. No biggie. On Monday afternoon, my cell phone breaks. It's been dropping calls for a few weeks, but now it won't stay connected to anyone. I don't have time to get another, so I just won't talk on the phone for a week. I have to work anyway.

Poison sumac spreads to look like a map of Italy, which suits.

On Tuesday, I'm low on groceries and down to take-out food, so I try to reheat pizza for dinner, but the oven won't go on. All right, no sweat, I can wait a week to get the oven fixed. I eat the pizza cold, which is delicious.

Poison sumac adds islands of Sicily and Sardinia, now geographically correct.

On Wednesday, I'm brewing my 55th cup of coffee and I go to get Half & Half from the refrigerator, but when I open the door, the light stays off. The refrigerator is on the fritz, and I notice water pooling on the floor. I can ignore the puddle, but the Half & Half will go bad and I need coffee.

Caffeine and deadline is my longest marriage.

So I call the appliance guys, and luckily the refrigerator guy is in the neighborhood, so he comes and replaces the gasket, whatever that is. I work all night on coffee adrenaline, and by Thursday morning I need breakfast, so I go to the freezer for ice cream.

Yes, you read that right. Ice cream for breakfast. On deadline, I crave sugar. Caffeine, sugar, and me are a threesome.

But when I open the freezer door, a solid block of ice coats the top shelf and my Häagen-Dazs is vanilla soup. I call the appliance guy again, and they tell me the gasket repair caused an air lock, whatever that is. They're not in the neighborhood and will get there when they can. So I drink the ice cream, and it's delicious. In fact, if I had cold pizza to go with my warm ice cream, I'd be in pig heaven.

Also, poison sumac has spread to the Italian island of Ischia, which sounds like "itchier" for a good reason.

On Friday, I'm working and adjusting to the new normal. My house is quiet because the radio stayed mute and the cell phone can't ring. I don't cook in the oven because it doesn't work, and there's no food left in the refrigerator, even though it does. I eat things that used to be frozen, like Boca Burgers, which I microwave for lunch and dinner. For breakfast I make toast. For dessert I have microwave popcorn, and it's all delicious. I'm backsliding with carbohydrates, like ex sex.

Carbs join sugar, caffeine, and me for the weekend. We have a deadline orgy.

Poison sumac invades Poland, intending world domination.

Saturday afternoon, my laptop is acting wacky. The monitor seems fainter and I can't read it, so I call my computer guy, who comes over. We use one of my old monitors with the laptop, but that doesn't work, so we replace the laptop with an old computer. This process takes four hours, during which I eat nothing but fingernails, for three more grams of carbohydrates.

Poison sumac marches westward to France. Paris is burning, and so is my chest.

Sunday morning, my throat aches and my tongue is swollen, but I'm fine. It hurts to eat anything, but that doesn't matter because there's nothing to eat. I can't drink either, but I'm out of coffee and running on bile. I power through to Monday morning, when I finally finish my book.

It's called *Think Twice*.

But it should have been called *Poison Sumac Acquires Nuclear Weapons*.

Booked

~~~~~~~~~

As you may know, my first book of adventures was entitled *Why My Third Husband Will Be a Dog.*

Which pretty much guaranteed that I'll never have a third husband, but you can't have everything. Mostly, I have fun.

I remember when I told Mother Mary that the book was going to be published. She was sitting at my kitchen island, her neat head bent over the crossword puzzle, her close-cropped hair showing a grayish whorl. A hearing aid nestled behind each ear like a plastic parenthesis. Next to her sat a mug of coffee, with a napkin covering the top. She always covers her drinks, perhaps to keep out airborne bacteria or incoming helicopters.

So I broke the news, and she looked up, lifting a sparse silver eyebrow.

"Why?" she asked.

"Why, what?"

"Why are they making a book about the stories? Who's gonna buy that?"

"I hope some people will. It's funny, right?"

"Yeah, but they already read them in the paper."

"Well, they might have missed some, or they might want

them all in one place, or they might give it as a present for the holidays."

She looked at me blankly, a slow blink of milky brown eyes, behind bifocals.

"Ma, not everybody lives in Philly and gets the *Inquirer*. You, for example, live in Miami."

"I don't need the paper, or the book. Cousin Nana tells me what it's about."

This is true. Never mind that the columns are online, so that Brother Frank can get one and print a copy for her, every Sunday. Instead, she prefers to rely on Cousin Nana from South Philly, and I have stopped pointing out that, in hearing "what it's about," she misses these superbly crafted sentences. I tried another tack:

"Ma, the cool thing is that you're going to be in a book. People will read about your lab coat and your traveling back scratcher. They'll know you hate Raquel Welch and love Omar Sharif. Aren't you excited?"

"No." She sniffs. "Who cares? Nobody cares."

"They do. At least, some of them do."

This is also true, if my email is any indication, and thank you for writing to me. Mother Mary always gets rave reviews. She's like the *American Idol* of mothers. Rather, the *Survivor* of mothers. Or maybe I'm the survivor.

Then I got another idea. "Ma, I'm going to have a few book signings, and you should come. I'm sure people would have questions for you, and you could answer them. Wouldn't that be fun?"

"No." She went back to her puzzle. "I'm not going."

"You could even sign the books."

"Why would I?"

I left it alone, knowing that it was too soon to start campaigning in earnest. Of course, in time, I guilted her into coming. After all, she's the reason I started writing, though she'll never know it from me, because Cousin Nana might forget to tell her this part. To explain, I've always loved this quote of Eleanor Roosevelt's: "A woman is like a tea bag. You never know how strong she is until she's in hot water."

I knew that was true, if only from living with Mother Mary, who had been in more hot water than any fifty tea bags and had come out stronger. Later, I saw that strength in my girlfriends, and I wanted to see in print the kind of women I saw in real life. I think of them as extraordinary, ordinary women. Tea bags, all.

Sisters to Nancy Drew.

That's why this book has the subtitle, The Amazing Adventures of an Ordinary Woman. I think it sums up the point, doesn't it?

So keep reading, and save your questions for Mother Mary. She has all the answers.

WordPerfect

~~~~~~~~~~

I think a lot about words, and I like to choose the most important words for the decades of my life.

For example, when I was in my twenties, everything was about dating, romance, and love. During school, I had crushes on anything that moved, and being Italian, I fell in love many times.

On the same day.

Just kidding.

But I did have a low flashpoint in those days, and the most important words of my twenties were, "I love you."

The words "I love you" lead to marriage, or at least they did then, and I had two of those in the next decade or so. And my most important words morphed from "I love you" to "I'm sorry."

I'm sure it's a coincidence.

In my thirties, I apologized for everything. I was like an apology machine. The apologies started with things like "I'm sorry I'm late," then increased to "I'm sorry I said what I said," and ended up with "I'm sorry I think what I think," "I'm sorry I am who I am," and ultimately, "I'm sorry I married you."

Really, really sorry.

Luckily, there were backsies.

This led to the most important words of my forties, which were, "Thank you." As in, "Thank you, God, for divorce."

Among so many other things.

I was thankful that I had gotten back on my feet and acquired a grace I should have had earlier. I was thankful for everything in my life. Thankful that Daughter Francesca was growing up so beautifully, despite the many curveballs I'd thrown her. Thankful for my parents, then both still alive. Thankful that I had my health, when so many did not. Thankful for my house, even with its mortgage. Thankful for my dogs, though they never listened. Thankful I had a second career, which I loved.

So what words are the most important for my fifties?

It's taken me years to figure it out, but I know it now. What's the word it's taken me this long to figure out, and once I figured it out, even longer to say out loud?

What is as important as "I love you," "I'm sorry," and "Thank you," now and forever?

Ask.

I never used to ask for anything. Help. An answer. A favor. A new job. A concession. A request.

Whatever it is, if I wanted it, I would never ask for it. I would just hope it came to me, magically. Or I might just suffer in silence, in the manner of the early Christian martyrs.

Heaven, help us.

Now I ask, and I get plenty of no's. But I've also gotten a yes or two, which feels like I won the lottery. There are a lot of little examples, but here's one: last weekend, I was at the National Book Festival, and I was scheduled to speak at breakfast. As book gigs go, this is a big one, but it was early in the morning.

I had to be dressed and ready by seven o'clock, and I was worried.

About my speech?

No.

About my hair.

I was going to speak in front of hundreds of people, so I wanted good hair. I called a few salons to see if I could get an appointment to get a blow-dry that morning, but the managers said they weren't open until seven o'clock, which was too late for me. So I asked:

"Sir, would you please come to my hotel room, for money?"

Well, not exactly, but you get the idea.

In my forties, I never would have asked. I would have gotten my hair blown-dry the day before the speech and slept all night in a chair, sitting up. In fact, I did do that once.

Please tell me I'm not alone.

But now, I ask for what I want.

The most they can do is say no, and they didn't. At six fifteen in the morning, a handsome young man arrived at my hotel room and blow-dried my hair. Honest to God, it was all I wanted from him, and that's what being fifty is all about.

Of course, I haven't forgotten, "Thank you."

And "I love you" will always matter.

But I'm not really sorry, at all.

Quirky

~~~~~~

By Francesca Scottoline Serritella

You know my mom is a bit eccentric, she'll come right out and tell you—that she shares the couch with five dogs, that she sleeps in her clothes for fun, that she eats the same three meals on rotation.

Did she tell you that one?

But she has some idiosyncrasies of which even she isn't aware. I think it's safe to say that I know her better than she knows herself, and none of them gets past me.

For one, my mom doesn't know how old I am.

I know it sounds impossible. I am her only daughter, and she loves me more than anything. She thinks she knows how old I am; if you ask her, she will deliver her answer with absolute certainty.

She'll just get it wrong.

I have no idea why this is. She is not some dumb blonde. In fact, she is a super-smart blonde. But just yesterday she sent me something she had just written about what she keeps on her refrigerator door. In it, she poked fun at how she can't bring herself to take down any of my old report cards, and she had the line, "As you may recall, she's 26 years old."

Fact: I am 24 years old.

She must have confused me with her other only child.

Mom's response? "When you're fifty-four years old, twenty-four and twenty-six aren't all that different."

Fair enough.

Generally, my mom is a tough cookie, but when it comes to recalling my age, she can be very suggestible. However old your kid is, that's how old I am. We were just recently in the supermarket, and we bumped into a woman she knew who mentioned, "Oh, my son is twenty," and my mom replied, "Get out! My daughter is the same age! We should set them up."

Again, 24 years old, here.

This isn't something that happened as she got older, either. She's had this quirk as long as I can remember. She kept pretty good track when I was under ten years old, but once you start adding dates and months into the mix, you're asking for trouble. When I began preschool, we had to bring in our birth certificates. It said my birthday was February 7, 1986.

For years, we had celebrated on February 6.

Oops.

One day off, what's the big deal?

At least it had the right name on it.

I also noticed my mom has developed a new mental blip. Sometimes, when she wants to say one thing, she'll say the opposite. But as I said, I know her inside out, backwards and forwards, so I've gained the uncanny ability to sense when it's Opposite Day.

She'll say, "I took the dogs out, Tony peed but Peach didn't."

"You mean Peach peed but Tony didn't?"

"That's what I said, isn't it?"

She truly doesn't know she does it. But that's part of her charm, and I know what she means anyway.

Another of my mom's charming quirks is she likes to sing around the house. But she doesn't sing whole songs, she sings the chorus of songs. To be specific, she sings the same few bars of the chorus, over and over and over again.

Now, you can imagine, if my mom can't remember my birthday, she's not much for lyrics, but she wouldn't let that stop her. She makes up her own lyrics about whatever's in front of her, which is usually one of the dogs. Since the *Mamma Mia!* movie came out two summers ago, her tune of choice has been "Money Money Money."

The hills are alive with the sound of ABBA.

But at this point, I don't think she remembers where the song came from, because, like I said, when she sings it, the lyrics might be:

"He's my, teeny tiny Tony, teeny tiny, he's my Tony dog!"

I could let this bother me, but then where would I be? She's so cheerful with her Tony songs, I'd be a jerk to come down on her. So it's developed into a call-and-response game. She sings the first line, and it's my job to come up with the next one, sung to the zippy rhythm of the electric guitar part. Put on the spot, I'll come up with something like, "He wants to eat that sandwich."

We're a regular Naomi and Wynonna Judd.

So even though I have to correct my mother on my age, translate her opposites, and listen to a broken record of ABBA's greatest hits, I don't really mind. To know someone is to know his or her quirks. To love someone is to *love* those quirks.

Or at least to sing along.

Nutty

Addictions sneak up on you. They lure you in, teasing you, and before you realize it, you have a craving you can't deny.

I'm talking, of course, about nuts.

I'm nuts about nuts.

It might be a seasonal thing. Come fall, I gather nuts with the single-mindedness of a backyard squirrel. I buy bags and bags, then settle down with the single-gal trifecta of a Diet Coke, a good book, and the nut du jour.

We're chasing the dragon, ladies.

My habit started when I was young, and my gateway drug was sunflower seeds. They're labor-intensive, which is nature's attempt at portion control.

Futile.

Nature's no match for me, jonesing for sunflower seeds.

Everybody eats sunflower seeds in different ways, and I split mine with my teeth, then amass a tiny pile, like a little gray treasure. When I have about twenty-five seeds, I shove them in my mouth, all at once. This very attractive process used to take me about ten minutes, but after years of practice, I've become a sunflower seed professional.

I can do twenty-five seeds in three minutes.

Don't try this at home. Or if you're married.

And I never cheat. That is, I never buy sunflower seeds already shelled. If I did, how else would I get that fine layer of filth under my fingernails?

Of course, no nut was as messy as the old-school pistachio, dyed red. I don't know who thought it made sense to dye pistachio nuts red, but I'm guessing it was the same guy who used to dye Easter chicks pink. You remember what would happen if you ate red pistachios. Your fingers would be red for days. It wasn't a nut, it was a tattoo.

When I was little, brother Frank and I used to eat tons of red pistachios, but that was before he was gay. I doubt he would do that, today. Gay men have too much style for pistachio fingers.

Plus nowadays we know that the red dye on pistachios causes cancer, or at least, a lifetime of celibacy, so we eat the normal brown kind. They're meaty and delicious, and many of them come out of the bag partway open, which is helpful. Occasionally you run across a closed pistachio, and if you do, here's my advice:

Move on.

There's nothing for you there.

Don't even try to open a closed pistachio. Tenacity doesn't begin to describe these hardy few. You could use a clam shucker, a blowtorch, or a nuclear weapon, but in the end, the closed pistachio will defeat you.

Instead, calm down and have an almond. It will take your mind off the closed pistachio, and it's always easy to crack, though it's disappointingly healthy. Walnuts fall into the same category. It's no fun to be addicted to something that's good for you.

Being addicted to something healthy is like loving exercise.

Go away.

Peanuts are also delicious, and because they properly belong in Snickers, they're naughty enough to qualify as an addiction. It was my beloved father who taught me to eat peanuts, by which I mean, he always ate the whole peanut, shell and all. It was the only way I knew to eat peanuts until one night, when I popped a whole peanut and everyone started pointing and laughing.

"You don't eat the shells, silly!" they all said.

So I stopped.

Not eating the shells, just eating the shells in public.

Love you, Dad.

My all-time favorite nut is the pumpkin seed, especially the kind that comes coated with hard salt, white as packed snow but with a higher sodium content. And they're so salty, they practically demand another Diet Coke, in a vicious, yet familiar, salt/sugar cycle. Once I start eating pumpkin seeds, I can't stop. They take as long as a sunflower seed to shell, yet are less satisfying, since the seed is merely a sliver. It has just enough meat to keep you wanting more, yet never enough to satisfy completely, even after twenty-five seeds.

Or fifty.

Pumpkin seeds are the crack cocaine of the nut world.

And I need an intervention.

Junk in the Trunk

~~~~~~~~~

If Freud wanted to know what women want, he could have asked. If he'd asked me, I would have answered:

Another kitchen cabinet.

And I just got one!

Here's how it happened.

It was about ten years ago that I remodeled my kitchen, adding white cabinets and a trash compactor. To tell the truth, I don't remember wanting a trash compactor and think it was Thing Two who wanted a trash compactor, but I've blamed enough on him, so let's just say I wanted a trash compactor.

At the time, my kitchen contractor said, "I'll install this trash compactor for you, but I bet you'll never use it."

"I'm sure I'll use it," said I. And I probably added, "Plus it will give me something to blame on somebody, down the line."

In any event, the trash compactor got installed, and it came with two free bags, which I promptly lost.

Ten years and one divorce later, it turns out that the contractor was right.

I should have married the contractor.

Anyway, I never used the trash compactor. Not once. I even forgot it was there until three months ago, when it began to emit a mysterious and foul odor. I searched the thing and could find no reason for it to be smelly, but I washed it inside and out anyway. Still the smell got worse and worse, until it was so bad I could barely eat in the kitchen. Then one day, the electrician came over to fix a light, and he said, "Smells like something died in here."

Bingo!

The electrician showed me that you could slide out the compactor, which I hadn't realized, and when we did, we found behind it an aromatic gray mound that used to be a mouse.

Eeek!

The electrician threw the dead mouse away, and I cleaned the trash compactor all over again, but it still stunk worse than my second marriage, which I didn't even think was possible, so I threw the trash compactor away, too.

Which left an oddly empty space on my kitchen island, a dark square among the white cabinets, like a missing front tooth.

I called the kitchen contractor, whose phone number I still had from ten years ago. As soon as he heard my voice, he said, "Told you," and came right over.

Last week he installed a new cabinet, including a drawer, then asked, "What are you going to use it for?"

"I'm not sure yet," I told him, excited by the possibilities. It was almost too much to hope for—a nice empty cabinet and a whole extra drawer. After he had gone, I pulled up a stool and contemplated my course of action.

The decision required me to consider the problem areas of my kitchen cabinets, which are many. My pot-and-pan cabinet is a mess because I hate to stack pots and pans in their proper concentric circles. I just pile them up any way, playing Jenga, only with Farberware. Also I can never figure out how to store pot lids, so I stick them in upside down, setting them wobbling on handles like the worst tops ever. Every time I open the cabinet door, they come sliding out like a stainless-steel avalanche.

I also have a cabinet containing Rubbermaid and Tupperware, but it's all mixed up, so that Rubbermaid lids are with Tupperware containers and Rubbermaid containers are with Tupperware lids, making the whole thing feel vaguely illicit, like an orgy of plastic products.

Then I have a cabinet of kitchen appliances I have never used once in my life but feel compelled to keep close at hand, namely a juicer, a waffle iron, and a SaladShooter.

You never know when you'll have to shoot a salad.

My kitchen drawers are equally problematic. I have one drawer for silverware and four others for junk, junk, junk, and junk. All the junk drawers contain the same junk, just more of it, namely, pens that don't work, pencils that have no points, extra buttons that go to clothes I've never seen, rubber bands I got free but can't part with, menus for restaurants I don't order from, and pennies.

In other words, it's all essential.

I think I know what to put in the empty cabinet.

Trash compactor bags.

Killer Apps

~~~~~~

Not only are my appliances breaking down, they're conspiring against me.

Or at least, though they claim to make my life easier, they really make it harder.

Observe.

I produce only seven dirty dishes a day—namely, one mug (morning coffee), three plates (breakfast, lunch, and dinner), three glasses (daily allotment of two Diet Cokes before forced by guilt to segue to tap water), and 56 spoons (for eating Häagen-Dazs out of the container).

I could wash my dishes in ten minutes, but I don't, because I have a beautiful dishwasher, now only one year old. I load it up every night and forget about the dirty dishes, only to unload them the next morning.

Even dirtier.

This goes on for a month. I'm convinced it's my imagination, but my glasses and dishes keep looking worse than when I put them in. I wrack my brain but can't figure it out, so I go through the good-girl checklist. Dishes rinsed off first? Check. Placed in rack properly? Check. Living a good and honest life? Check.

Yet my dishes remain filthy. I give up and call the appliance guy. He examines the dishwasher, then asks, "Do you use a drying agent?"

"A what?" Evidently not.

He points to a mysterious hole in the dishwasher door. "That's what this is for. You put the drying agent in here. It will prevent the buildup from the water."

Now they tell me. "Why didn't I know about drying agents?"

"It's in the owner's manual. Did you read it?"

"Does it have a car chase?"

He doesn't answer.

"Then, no."

He adds, "You can buy a drying agent in any grocery store, and you should also pick up a dishwasher cleaning agent."

I try to follow. "My dishwasher needs to be cleaned?"

"Sure."

"But isn't it supposed to wash things?"

"Yes."

"So why doesn't it just wash itself?"

He gathers my question is rhetorical, which it isn't, and I walk him to the door, cranky. I have to buy dishwashing powder, a drying agent, and a dishwashing washing agent—all to clean seven dishes? What does the dishwasher do to earn its keep? If you ask me, somebody's slacking and his name rhymes with KitchenAid.

My clothes dryer isn't pulling its weight, either. For the past year, I have to put it through two cycles to dry anything, and if you think I use only a few dishes, I won't even tell you how often I wash my sheets. Generally, I wait for the dogs to complain.

Anyway I call the appliance guy and he says the clothes dryer is fine, but I need to clean the outtake hose because of the buildup.

Buildup again! "What buildup? There's no water there."

"No, but there's humid air."

"Air can build up?" I ask him, incredulous.

"Or lint. Check the owner's manual, you'll see."

Now I hate the owner's manual more than I hate the buildup.

And don't get me started on lighting timers.

In a fit of temporary insanity, I had timers installed on the lights at my front door, back door, and garage. The electrician stuck these very tasteful white things into my light switches, and they'd be great if they worked, but they don't. Their second day on the job, they joined the appliance conspiracy, so I can never guess what time they'll go on or off. Now the front lights go on at three o'clock in the afternoon and go off at nightfall, like accomplices to all burglars in the tristate area.

Plus the garage light goes on at two in the morning, just in time to wake me and the dogs up, so we can all bark for the next hour, when we fall into an exhausted sleep.

I would turn the lights on and off manually, but the fancy timer switches won't let me do that. They're the control freaks of the electrical world.

I can't even claw them out of the switchplate, nor do they respond to profanity and other forms of verbal abuse.

Now the only thing building up is my blood pressure.

A Paid Political Announcement

I've lived through a number of elections by now, and they get more and more negative.

I try to stay positive about negative ads.

Why? Because I write fiction for a living, and so do the people who write these ads. The truth can be so boring when you don't make it up.

I also appreciate a good laugh, and I laugh every time one of those ads comes on. And wouldn't you rather see a good, old-fashioned smear of a political ad than yet another commercial for Cialis? Evidently, the stock market isn't the only thing going down.

It doesn't matter which candidate you support, or party you belong to. Negative ads are always the same. My favorite negative ads are about candidates running for the state offices, whatever they are. I never heard of any of these guys, but now I know they're liars, thieves, wastrels, killers, and closet watchers of *Project Runway*.

I don't know them, but already I hate them and am afraid of them. A scarier lot you never saw, and if they get elected, they'll bankrupt the entire world.

Oops, too late.

Sometimes I like to imagine what the negative ads for other politicians would have been. Consider, for example, the original change candidates, the Founding Fathers.

You say you want a revolution?

Take George Washington. The negative ads would tell you he had wooden teeth. Would you really vote for a man who doesn't floss? Plus I heard he got that tall by taking steroids. The battle of Valley Forge wasn't bravery, it was 'roid rage.

And how about an ad for Thomas Jefferson? Dude had a ponytail, wore ruffled shirts, and spent way too much time in Paris. You know what I'm saying. Don't ask, don't tell that there were Manolos in his armoire.

Ben Franklin. So he invented the printing press in his basement. You know what else he was making down there? Bombs, meth, and counterfeit copies of *Sex and the City II.*

So you see how much fun you can have, making negative ads for heroes. Some people would call that libelous and disrespectful, but they can't take a joke.

Plus you have to look for the silver lining in the negative ads, and by that I mean that they create jobs for so many people.

First, the scary voice-over people. You know who I mean. The whispery female voice threatening that the Democrat will spend us into oblivion, and the deep, rich bass of the man who warns that the Republican will send us to war, armed only with duct tape. You don't hear those scary ads except at election time, and those voice-over people need work.

The rest of the year, it's the perky types who get the voice-over jobs, like the housewife voices happy about floor wax or the hubby voices happy about car wax. If it weren't for negative ads, you would get the idea that the only difference between women and men is what they wax.

Plus, what about bad photographers? Negative ads give them the only work they get. They're the ones who take the terrible photos of the candidate, or catch their ugliest moments. And think of the horror music people. The other day, I heard the most terrifying music ever coming from the TV, but it wasn't an ad for the sequel to *Saw* or even a rerun of *Jaws*. It was a candidate for state senate. Nothing like a scary drumbeat to make you think of nuclear war, serial murder, or politics.

Scary voice-over people, bad photographers, and horror music composers would be out of a job but for negative ads.

So there you have it.

Democracy creates jobs, and negative ads are proof.

Angie The Kitchen Aid

This is a world in which the squeaky wheel gets the grease, but I'm wondering if we should change that.

Tell you what happened.

It was a typical afternoon chez Scottoline, and I was working in my kitchen office, which is a euphemism for the computer nearest the refrigerator.

My favorite place to work, for obvious reasons.

Anyway, the kitchen was quiet except for the thrumming of the dishwasher, which was running for the second time that day, because I was trying to get the glasses clean. If you recall, I've been having dishwasher drama, and it turns out that all the rinsing agents in the world have failed me. It was making me crazy, a mystery I couldn't solve. My glasses were cloudy enough to be a weather report.

To stay on point, I was working happily, surrounded by the dogs. Little Tony sat in my lap, because he always begs to come up. Ruby The Crazy Corgi was at my feet, since she usually curls up there. Penny, my younger golden retriever, was sitting beside me, pawing to be petted, which is her habit. Only Angie, my older golden, was on her own, lying near the dishwasher, probably because it was warm. Angie is soft, fluffy, and plump, with fur the toasty hue of vanilla wafers, and all she was doing was watching me, resting her head on her paws, her brown eyes dark as bittersweet chocolate in a mask gray with age. She didn't paw, scratch, or whine. She asked for nothing.

I caught her eye, and she flopped her tail once, letting it *thwap* on the hardwood floor, because all it takes to make Angie happy is to look in her direction. And because she never asks for anything, she doesn't get very much. She's twelve years old and she comes on our daily walks when she's up for it, but she doesn't get the attention the pushy ones do.

Angie isn't a squeaky wheel.

But that day, seeing her by herself, I finally focused on her and realized that I had been neglecting her. Just because she didn't ask for attention didn't mean she didn't deserve it, or need it. She's a great old dog, even more precious because she won't be around forever.

So I lifted Little Tony from my lap, stepped over Ruby, ignored Penny, and went over to Angie. I sat down on the floor beside her, gave her a big kiss, and scratched behind her ear while she drifted off into a noisy slumber.

And of course I began to relax, too, in a deep, centered way, and I realized that that was the gift you get from a dog like Angie. Because she's at peace with herself, she makes you at peace with yourself. It made me understand that I'm rarely spending time doing something as simple as petting a sleeping dog, and that I'm too often running in all directions, responding to the ring of cell phones, the beep of incoming email, and the latest text in my BlackBerry.

Angie made me take a break.

I enjoyed the moment, letting my gaze wander over the

things I see every day in the kitchen, like the baby photographs of Daughter Francesca, the bamboo plant on the windowsill, and a crumpled tube of toothpaste, near the sink. I brush my teeth three times a day, like a good girl, and about two months ago, I started keeping a toothbrush and toothpaste downstairs, because I got too lazy to keep running upstairs.

Then, in a blink, it struck me.

I'd been brushing my teeth in the kitchen sink, and that residual toothpaste must have been going down the drain, which flowed to the same pipe that feeds water to the dishwasher.

Angie The Kitchen Aid.

In other words, there's nothing wrong with my KitchenAid, there's something wrong with me. If I stop brushing my teeth in the kitchen sink, the clouds should clear from my glassware.

Mystery solved.

And all because I finally took the time to think, thanks to a sweet old golden retriever.

Angie.

Book Party

I'm grateful to my readers, so every year I have a contest for book clubs who read my latest book, as a thank-you to them. They enter the contest by sending me a picture with their members holding up my book. The winner is chosen at random, and the prize is dinner with me.

I'm more fun than you think, okay?

The consolation prize is even better. Everybody who enters the contest gets to come to a big party at my house. I've been doing this for four years now, and we have a great time, eating, drinking, and yapping away.

It's mostly women, except for a few enlightened men. Chocolate flows like wine. Well, if chocolate could flow, it would.

What really flows is estrogen.

We start out talking about books and end up talking about our husbands, dogs, children, hair, and carbohydrates.

Fun for girls!

By way of background, the first year I gave the book club party, there were 100 people. My assistant Laura and I ordered some pastries, served it ourselves on paper plates, and made coffee in two electric urns that blew every fuse in my house.

It was what they call a soft opening. Perhaps because you have to be soft in the head to open that way.

The second year, 200 people came, and I hired a caterer and rented a tent. The book club party turned professional, and we got our act together.

The third year, 300 people came, and I kept the same caterer and rented a larger tent. All good.

The fourth year, which is this year, guess how many people entered the contest and said they were coming to the book club party?

Given the pattern, you would think 400, right?

Me, too.

But the answer was 700.

OMG.

This is a good problem to have, because it means that more book clubs are reading my books, but at first I didn't know what to do. I called Laura in a panic. I wailed, "What do we do?"

"We remain calm."

"Speak for yourself."

"We'll be fine."

I wanted to believe her. Laura is always right, and she knows when to panic. The answer is never. She's the mother of two little boys and she never, ever panics. But I'm me.

"No, we won't be fine." I was freaking. "We can't change the date and split the party up over two days, can we?"

"This late?"

"Then I'm praying for rain."

"God forbid, " Laura said, but I didn't listen.

I prayed very, very hard.

Harder than I'd prayed for a pony when I was little.

I didn't think I could fit 700 people in and around my house, and even if I could, I wouldn't get to meet and hang with my guests the way I like, which is the whole point of the event. In fact, I always greet every guest as they arrive, and Laura and I figured that if I spent only a minute with each person, at 700 people, it would take—

Well, you can do the math.

I can't. It gives me the heebee-jeebies.

So I prayed for rain, and we ordered a tent that would house a circus, doubled the food order, and nixed the hot drinks, even though it was October and chilly.

I'm an author, not a restaurant.

I watched the weather reports. They were talking rain, and my spirits lifted. I hate to say it, but I hoped it would keep a few people away. But two days before the party, the forecast was for a nor'easter, which would keep more than a few people away. And then there were reports of a second nor'easter, which would hit at the same time.

In other words, the perfect storm was going to hit my book club party.

Be careful what you wish, right?

I called Laura in a bigger panic. "I'm so sorry I prayed for rain. They're talking gale-force winds. Twenty-degree temperatures. Tons of rain."

"Don't worry."

"Will the tent blow away? How will we get the food truck through the mud? Where will we park the cars?

"It will all work out okay."

Well, what do you think happened?

Did the two nor'easters come as predicted?

Was it a disaster?

Yes, and no.

Laura was right, yet again.

Two nor'easters did strike, converging right over my tent, which withstood the high winds and torrential rain. The food truck got through the mud, we covered the grass with hay, and a little over half the crowd showed up. I was able to greet every one of my guests, and give out more than a few hugs.

Yay!

We all had a great time, not just despite the storm, but because of it, and the hardy few that made it to the party proved they were the type of women that I admire and write about—strong, resilient, and fun.

Like Eleanor Roosevelt said, "A woman is like a tea bag. You never know how strong she is until she's in hot water."

Well, these women were tea bags, to the max.

And what happened to me?

I'm praying for George Clooney.

Big Pimpin' on Thanksgivin'

This Thanksgiving, I'm pimping out my family.

My first book of adventures was published two days before Thanksgiving. I did a short tour for the book and thought it would be a great idea to get Mother Mary to come along to a few signings, because she gets more fan mail than I do.

By the way, the order of email love goes: Mother Mary, Daughter Francesca, Little Tony, and me.

I'm good with that.

In fact, I agree.

Mother Mary said she'd shill for me in return for her free Thanksgiving dinner. She also agreed to stay at my house through December, though I won't make her sell books on Christmas. She's eighty-six, and you can lash your mother only so much.

On Christmas, I'll give her the day off.

So she can cook.

Santa might not approve, though if he reads me, he knows that I'm the Nice one and she's straight-up Naughty.

But arrangements need to be made to fly her up from Miami, namely a single reservation, which for some reason necessitates five phone calls, with much discussion about the best day to travel. I want her to come up on November 20th.

"Why so early?" she asks. "I'm busy."

"Doing what?"

"None of your business"

I beg to differ. Actually it is my business. It is exactly my business. "Okay, when can you come up?"

"Earliest is the 22nd."

"How about the 20th?"

"The 22nd."

"How about the 21st? We can relax a little before the book tour."

"The 22nd is fine."

I give up. My mother could negotiate peace in Iraq, Afghanistan, and the Middle East, all at once. She'd make them surrender. She'd take their guns and stop making their women wear burkas. Which reminds me that Mother Mary has been known to don a lab coat, impersonating Dr. Bunsen Honeydew, so I ask, "Ma, what are you going to wear to the signings?"

"Why do you want to know?"

"What about your lab coat? You're leaving that at home, right?"

"Of course. I don't wear that in public."

"Okay." Just checking. Then I reconsider. "On second thought, maybe you should bring the lab coat. You could wear it to the signings. That would be cute. If they read me, they know you're an amateur doctor."

Silence.

I remain undaunted. My imagination takes over. The notion of dressing my mother up for a signing strikes me as marketing genius, so I try to convince her: "Ma, we could get you a toy stethoscope. A fake prescription pad. You could prescribe meatballs. You could be your own health insurance company, called Independence Blue Cross-To-Bear."

Suddenly I realize that she's not quiet, but the call got dropped. For a minute, I wonder if she hung up on purpose, but that's not her style. Now the fun begins, because if I'm on the phone with anyone other than my mother and a call gets dropped, somebody calls somebody else back, no big deal.

But not Mother Mary.

Usually, it takes her ten minutes to realize that the call was dropped, during which I try to call her back five times, each time getting her voicemail. Then, an hour later, when we finally reconnect, our discussion will always go like this, as it does this time:

"So, Ma, I was saying that—"

"What happened?" she asks.

"The call got dropped."

"I didn't hear you anymore."

"I know. It disconnected."

"Did you hang up?"

"No, it's just dropped. Calls gets dropped."

"Why?"

"I don't know." Mind you, she's not confused. She's angry. A dropped call is either a personal affront or a government wiretap.

"We shoulda kept the Jitterbug. You said this new phone would work, but it doesn't."

"It does, but calls get dropped. Just because the call gets dropped doesn't mean the phone doesn't work." As soon as I finish saying it, it sounds ridiculous. A phone costs plenty, so maybe it's reasonable to expect it to work, but never mind, I have to get the Thanksgiving conversation back on track.

But to fast-forward, I don't. We never recover from the mystery of the dropped call.

So you know where this is going.

Mother Mary will come visit, we'll go to a few book signings, and we'll celebrate Thanksgiving.

And you know what I'm thankful for.

Another holiday with my family.

Especially Dr. Bunsen Honeydew.

Some Enchanted Evening

By Francesca Scottoline Serritella

My grandmother, whom you know as Mother Mary, just turned eighty-six years old, and so I gave her a call. I sang Happy Birthday, we discussed the usual topics, and then she asked me one of the questions she always asks: "Kitten, are you having fun?" And for once, I had a real story for her.

I answered, "I had the best night of my life."

Last weekend, my cousin invited me to a charity ball. I expected it to be a formal, bordering on stuffy, occasion, one that intimidated me. But I had a red dress in my closet, and sometimes that is reason enough.

The night turned out to live up to every possible promise a red dress can make. The event was held in a beautiful, old New York building. There, I met a British man who was so handsome, so debonair, I could hardly speak when he started talking to me, much less move when he asked me to dance.

He led me to the dance floor, where we remained for the next two hours. He spun me around like a pro, and on the last beat of every song, he'd toss me into the most daring, thrilling dips, the sort of trust-me-or-die, hair-grazes-the-floor dips that make other people stop and look.

A group of us, including Prince Charming, ended the night

at an authentic piano bar—a tiny place where a gifted pianist played song after song and the waitress and bartender took turns singing long after last call.

Finally, it was time for me to bid my reluctant farewells. I stepped outside and saw that my golden coach was once again a yellow taxi, and the evening rain had released smells of the city not found in fairy tales.

Driving home, replaying the evening in my mind, I could barely believe such a night could be real. As I stepped out of the cab, I looked down at my feet and saw that both of my shoes had an ugly bit of glue exposed over the peep-toe. And then I realized I had my proof that the night had really happened:

I had danced the bows off my shoes.

"Oh, Kitten, that's marvelous!" my grandmother cried. Her tone turned serious, "But did you sing at the piano bar?"

I laughed. "No."

"*No?* Why not?"

"Oh, I don't know, I'd be too embarrassed. I don't think I even know all the words to any song."

"You know *all* those Sinatra songs! I always used to sing at piano bars when I was young. Anywhere I went, if there was a piano, I would sing. You see, I was a bit of a show-off then."

"Oh yeah?"

"*Oh* yeah! I would go to a party in a great dress, and I'd dance all night in the center of the room, and I'd always sing at a piano. That was sixty, seventy years ago, but I loved it. You should never be embarrassed. You should have sung your heart out."

The picture she was painting of herself was far different from the grandmother I knew, but it was one I could see clearly. I realized that inside the woman who survived an impoverished childhood, who selflessly raised two kids and worked when few women did, who, despite arthritic fingers and worsening eyesight, can still assemble one hundred perfect ravioli on any given afternoon, was a woman who loved the limelight, who could dance all night, and who sang at a piano, always.

We said goodbye, and when I hung up the phone I had a different perspective on my night at the ball. At the time, I had tried my hardest to live in the moment, to savor every minute of that night. The next day, I had rushed to tell my friends before I forgot a detail. I'd even been tempted to write it down in a journal, get it on the record, anything to preserve a magical evening that was over too soon. But now I know that it was a night I will carry with me. A night I will tell my grandchildren about—the night I danced the bows off my shoes.

I know I will remember that night, because my grandmother still does. But the next time I'm in a piano bar, I'll sing.

Big

The holidays are coming, and I have an annual tradition of buying the house a Christmas present. For example, last year I bought the house a puppy.

I never got a thank-you note.

I keep thinking about getting the house another puppy, but this year I got it something it wanted more, which was delivered this morning.

Here's what happened.

I have a 32-inch TV in an entertainment center that's across the room from the couch, and as the years go by, the TV's been getting smaller and smaller, and harder and harder to see.

I'm not getting older.

My TV is shrinking.

Maybe someone left it out in the rain, like the cake in that song, or maybe someone put it in the dryer, I don't know. But I'd been thinking that this Christmas, I'd buy the house a big TV.

I'd been holding off because I didn't want the hassle, and I knew it would be expensive, because whenever I look at the little ones, they seem fairly costly. In the past, I'd gotten free little TVs, using the reward points from a credit card on which I charge the other things the house wants, like handbags and shoes.

In other words, I'd been stalling on the big TV, and all the big TVs in the reward catalog cost a billion more points than I had, so I bit the bullet. I drove to the store, drawn to the TV department, eyes agog. It was dark, lit on all four sides by screens, like a TV cave. All of the TVs, from floor to ceiling, were tuned to the same football game, which was humongous.

I stared astounded as a football flew by, big as an airbus. Linemen tall as Godzilla crashed into other helmeted monsters, like worlds colliding. Gigantic cheerleaders jumped and yelled, their mouths big as swimming pools, and their breasts, well, you get the idea.

Wow.

Jeez.

There was enough plastic in those babies to keep all of us fresh for days.

In other words, everything on the big TVs was BIG.

Plus the colors were as vivid and pretty as flowers. The yellow in the team uniforms was bright marigold, the orange like Gerber daisies. I spotted blood on a jersey, red as a geranium. It was the most floral violence ever.

I fell in love.

Or rather, my house did.

It knew that it had made the right decision to stop being such a cheapskate and come to the big TV store. Its good judgment was confirmed when it looked around and noticed that none of the TVs was as tiny as the one at home, its ex-TV.

Then the question became which type of big TV to get, among the dizzying array of plasma TVs, LCD TVs, LED-LCD TVs, rear projection TVs, and tube TVs, whatever that is. I had no idea what I had at home, or what to choose, but a salesgirl told me that if your room has lots of windows, go with LCD, which probably stands for large colossal something.

So then the only question was, how large and colossal?

I had gone into the store thinking that a 42-inch TV would be big enough, because I wanted to keep it classy and tasteful. But all of a sudden, the 42-inch looked so puny, next to the 48-inch.

And the price wasn't as bad as I thought it would be. Plus classy and tasteful is overrated, so I settled on the 48-inch.

Until I caught sight of the 52-inch.

Which was bigger.

And on sale.

In fact, the 52-inch cost less than the 48-inch, which I didn't understand, because the 52-inch offered four extra inches of multicolored bigness.

So the 52-inch started to make sense to me.

Er, the house.

And the 52-inch was so gorgeous and easy to see, like Large Print TV. I was sure it wouldn't shrink for a long, long time. So I bought it, and they delivered it this morning.

With a crane.

It's so huge it doesn't fit in the entertainment center. In fact, it barely fit in the front door.

It stands in its immense box in the family room, blocking the view of the Christmas tree, towering over the couch and chairs, like a monolith at Stonehenge. The cats and dogs sniff it in fear, and I don't know whether to worship it or return it.

But I have a feeling I'll just open it and watch it.

Forever.

Big love, from me and mine, to you and yours.

Family Photo

It's a wonder that any family survives its family photo. The Flying Scottolines almost didn't.

The blame begins and ends with me, and you'll see why.

The whole thing was my idea in the first place. Mother Mary and Daughter Francesca were both at my house, visiting for the Christmas holidays. At the same time, I had to do a photo shoot for my website, so I was wearing my new red-striped sweater and having a photographer over. Plus I had gotten my hair blow-dried professionally.

Professional hair, new clothes, and a camera is a harmonic convergence for girls.

But first I needed cooperation from Mother Mary.

What were the odds?

I turned to her, explained the situation, and asked her if she wanted to take a family photo.

"Why would I?" she asked, looking up from her crossword. She was wearing her lab coat, which is her idea of loungewear.

"For fun. How often are we all together like this? If we wear something red, we could send out a Christmas card with a picture of us on it."

"Who needs that?"

"We do," I said, firmly. When I put on my firm voice, she knows I mean business. Also she was at my mercy, because I would withhold food and water. "And you can't wear your lab coat."

She lifted a gray eyebrow. "Why not?"

"Because it's not red, you're not a doctor, and it makes you look crazy."

She didn't laugh, and I marched her upstairs, changed her three times, and got her dressed with only a minor fistfight. Francesca was her usual cooperative self, so she showered and changed into a red sweater in no time, then even made me up, because she's a born makeup artist. When I apply my eyeliner, it looks like an EKG.

Francesca turned to Mother Mary, mascara wand in hand. "Want me to make you up, too?"

"Why do I need makeup?"

"So you look good for the photo."

"I look fine."

"You do, but with the flash, you need a little makeup."

"Hmph," my mother said, submitting only because it was Francesca who asked. If it had been me, she would have stabbed me with the eyepencil.

So we all got pretty in our red sweaters and sat down on the couch in a straight line, like superannuated triplets. The dogs gathered at our feet in a way they don't in real life, as they are camera hounds.

Sorry.

So the photographer snaps a few pictures and shows them

to us, and we all notice that light is reflecting off my mother's glasses, so you can't see her eyes.

I say, "Ma, you have to take your glasses off."

"How am I supposed to see?"

"It's easy." I pluck the glasses from behind her ears, fold them up, and set them aside. "Just look at the lens of the camera."

"What if I can't find it?"

The photographer answers helpfully, "I'll wave my hand, and you can look at that."

"Thanks," I say, but Mother Mary remains doubtful, as she sinks back onto the couch.

The photographer starts snapping away again, then shows us the pictures, and this time, we all notice that Mother Mary is not smiling.

"Ma," I say to her, "why aren't you smiling?"

"Why should I?"

"Ma, you have to smile."

Francesca puts a gentle hand on my mother's shoulder. "You look so nice when you smile. Just smile, okay?"

"Hmph," my mother says again, then we all take our seats, a few photos are snapped, and the photographer shows them to us. Again, we all notice that my mother isn't smiling enough. Francesca and I are beaming, and my mother looks a little gassy.

"Ma, you have to smile more."

"I can't smile any more."

"Yes, you can. Show your teeth."

"What's that mean?"

"Say cheese."

Mother Mary means it when she says "cheese."

My mother rolls her eyes. "What am I, a baby?"

Evidently, I think but don't say, and we all sit back down.

An exhausting two hours later, we look at the photos, which have turned out terribly. Francesca and I are smiling, but my mother appears to be snarling. The camera seems to have caught her with the *ch* part of cheese, instead of the *eese.* Her teeth are showing like a wolf with dentures.

But that's not the real problem. With all the focus on Mother Mary, we have failed to notice that I'm having a wardrobe disaster. The stripes running across my chest aren't straight, like they were when the sweater was on the hanger. Instead, the lines run up my chest and down again, sagging at the ends, like a frown.

Bottom line, I'm a middle-aged woman, and my sweater has busted me.

Again, sorry.

Christmas card photos are so much fun.

We really do love each other. Really.

"Oh no," I wail, and Francesca puts an arm around me.

"It's not you, it's the bra."

My mother comes over, puts her glasses back on, and checks the pictures.

And smiles, ear-to-ear.

Mother Mary Becomes
A Rock Star

I'm back from book tour, and here's the recap:

The crowds were happy to see Francesca and me, but they were happier to see Mother Mary. Even though she's eighty-six, she made it to every nighttime event for ten days. And, yes, she wore her lab coat and wielded her back scratcher like a scepter, to thunderous applause.

Of course, it went to her little gray head. By the second

Mother Mary rocks the crowd in her lab coat.

signing, she wanted a limo, and by the third, a cut of the royalties.

I told her to get an agent.

At each signing, she wowed everybody with the story of how she became Earthquake Mary, when she was the only person in South Florida who felt an earthquake that happened 300 miles away from her, in Tampa. I wrote about that in one of my stories, but I'm not sure anyone believed it until they heard it from the horse's mouth. And of course, when I gave her the microphone, I couldn't get it back.

At one bookstore, I physically had to wrest it from her tiny grasp. There's nothing like a karate chop to your aged mother to warm a crowd.

Not only did she tell stories, she signed books. At many stores, the audience numbered as many as two hundred people, and Mother Mary signed every book in her adorably shaky script. She also took the time to meet everybody, kiss cheeks, and give out Tastykakes, which is my thank-you gift to my readers, because she taught me that if you love people, you feed them saturated fats.

She was on her best behavior. She made faces behind my back only once. Her single slip was when she met an elegant woman reader who asked her if she was really eighty-six, and Mother Mary answered, "Yes, and still horny!"

After that, I cautioned against the Dirty Grandma routine, in no uncertain terms. Raising your parent is harder than raising your child.

Francesca, of course, behaved flawlessly. She did more than her share, even wrangling the dogs. We brought Little Tony and Pip, though we didn't make them wear lab coats.

Also we couldn't find any small enough.

Francesca gave a speech about why she loves to write and answered each question with typical grace. In other words, she told the audience that I was a great mother and didn't say that we had eaten dinner at McDonald's four nights in a row.

Nor did she mention that I didn't give the dogs a bathroom break because it would cost me book sales.

I'm an animal lover until my mortgage is involved.

Then they hold it in.

When the tour ended, Mother Mary said it made her feel like "a rock star," so imagine my surprise when she announced that she wanted to return to Miami early.

"Really?" I asked her. "Why?"

"I'm cold, what do you think?"

"I'll turn up the heat," I said, but it was already set at 73 degrees. Even the cats were having hot flashes.

"It won't help. I want to go home."

"But you're supposed to stay for Christmas."

"Sorry, I'd rather be warm. Who needs winter?"

I tried not to take it personally and had her at the airport the next day, where I got all teary. It wasn't until the drive home that I realized I shouldn't be sad. Francesca would be home for Christmas, and there were plenty of families who wouldn't be together at the holiday. I thought of people who had lost family members they loved, and still others who had family serving in Afghanistan, Iraq, and all around the world.

We would all be alone, together.

And that's not what family is about, anyway.

Family may not be there on the holiday, but they'll be there when you need them, like on book tour.

The family tour.

Family will help you out, even if it means eating a bag of cold French fries in a car, after a three-hour book signing.

At age eighty-six.

So to those of you who won't be with your family this holiday, I share your pain—and your love.

Family is with us whenever it really matters.

And the rest of the time, they're inside.

Happy Holidays, with love, to you and your family.

Unexpected

~~~~~~~

Let me tell you about the great gift I got this past Christmas, and it's one that didn't come with a bow.

It changed the way I think about my life.

I didn't expect I would get this gift, going in. The day didn't end like it started out, at all.

Which is kind of the point.

By way of background, you should know that Daughter Francesca and I have spent every Christmas together ever since she was one, when Thing One and I divorced. She would spend Christmas Eve with him, and the day with me, and we were all happy about that, or at least as happy as anybody can be when their kid has to split herself in two.

But Francesca is older now, and this past Christmas she decided to spend the day with her father because they were visiting his family. I wasn't happy about that, but I tried not to grumble too loudly, and you can imagine how well that worked. Me, shutting up about my feelings?

Me, shutting up at all?

So you know the answer:

Girlfriends!

I called my best friend Franca and whined. I always think

that if I killed somebody, Franca would help me hide the body, but so far I haven't killed anybody and I'll probably never get the chance.

Which means that most of the time, Franca has to listen to me whine.

But this time she also solved the problem.

She's divorced, too, and to my surprise, she told me that her kids would be spending Christmas with their father, although she had a better attitude about it than I, as she does in all things.

So we hatched a plan. We both love Meryl Streep and had been dying to see *It's Complicated,* which was opening on Christmas, so we decided to go.

It's not how I'd ever spent Christmas, but I met Franca at the theater, and lo and behold, it was almost full. We settled into our seats with popcorn, Diet Coke, and Raisinets, and I started to feel a little better. The crowd was in a holiday mood, and when I looked around, it was almost all middle-aged women like us. No surprise, as the movie is a total chick flick and we were all girl-crushing on Meryl.

So we were enjoying the movie, which, as you may know, is about a divorced woman who has an affair with her ex-husband. And about halfway through, there's a scene in which Meryl Streep's character gets wistful and says something to the effect that, "every divorced women wonders if she should get back with her ex-husband."

At which point the audience exploded into laughter.

It wasn't supposed to be a funny line, but it cracked everybody up, and somebody shouted at the screen, "Oh, no, they don't!"

Which renewed the gales of laughter.

That was the moment I realized that I could very well be sitting in an audience of women who were probably divorced, whose kids were spending Christmas with their fathers, and who had come to the movie with their divorced girlfriends to see a movie about everybody's favorite divorced girlfriend.

And none of us wanted to get back with our ex-husbands.

Not for one minute.

It took a while for the laughter to die down, but eventually it did, and when the movie ended, we all went home to our lives.

I had learned a lesson, which took me this long to understand.

It's all about expectations.

I never expected how my life would turn out. That fact comes into relief on holidays, because they're the time when expectations are front and center, and all divorced people have different holidays than they expected.

I'm not saying we have better or worse, I'm just saying that they're not what we expected.

And I learned on Christmas that that's okay.

I can live with that, and so can Franca, and so can the forty or so women in the theater that day.

Because we can still laugh and be happy, but in a different way.

Best gift ever.

Happy Holidays, year 'round.

UnResolutions for the New Year

~~~~~~~~

Time for my annual UnResolutions lecture. If you don't know how this goes, I'm trying to change the way everybody in the world does things.

Now you see why I'm divorced. Twice.

Here's what I mean.

In the real world, everybody makes resolutions for the New Year, i.e., things they don't like about themselves and need to change. For example, I'd love to lose some weight, so I resolve not to eat chocolate cake.

Impossible. Wrong-headed. Dumb.

God wouldn't have invented chocolate cake if he didn't want us to eat it. Therefore, ipso fatso, resolutions are a waste of time.

And they're so negative. Why even make a mental list of all the things you hate about yourself? Why start the New Year keeping all of your faults firmly in mind?

I have a better idea.

Flip it.

Hence, the UnResolution.

Think back to the things you've been doing this past year which make you happy and which you intend to keep doing. Come up with your own list of UnResolutions, and there's no limit on the number of great things you can think about yourself. In fact, I hope you have a long list of reasons for your own awesomeness. Anything qualifies, even if it sounds odd or weird. In fact, especially if it sounds odd or weird.

This isn't counting your blessings, exactly. It's more like counting your eccentricities. As you will see below, with mine.

UnResolution Number One: I resolve not to wash my hair. By way of background, I used to wash my hair every day, like the shampoo commercials say, but nowadays, I wash my hair once a week and national holidays. And you know what? It looks better. And not in that too-cool-for-school dirty-hair way, but just healthier. Shinier.

Well, shinier, for sure.

Bottom line, washing your hair every day isn't great for hair as "highlighted" as mine, which is euphemistic for bleached into blond obedience. So I resolve to keep my hair dirty this year.

Thus ensuring my single status.

UnResolution Number Two. I resolve to keep watching the same movies over and over because I love them. Now this is going to sound crazy, but I love to have movies on TV while I work, especially movies like *The Godfather*. I have seen *The Godfather* probably 145 times, yet I watch it every time cable shows a marathon. Bottom line, one of the great things about living alone is that no one is around to say, "You're not going to watch *The Godfather* again, are you?"

Answer: You're darn tootin'. I'm going to watch it until I have it memorized and then some. And I'm going to love every minute.

And *The Godfather*'s not alone. I'm talking *Donnie Brasco*.

Mamma Mia! Something's Gotta Give. What About Bob? The Birdcage. Analyze This. There are so many movies I love, and if they're on TV, I'm watching them. And I'm going to keep watching them, over and over, all year.

UnResolution Number Three: I resolve to keep my car too clean. I love my car, which now has over 100,000 miles. It's as white as a bar of Ivory soap, and I love how it looks when it's clean, so I get it cleaned a lot. This may be because all I have to do is sit on my butt and drive it through a car wash. If they had a House Wash, my house would be immaculate.

When my car is clean, I feel an unaccountable surge in self-esteem, as if a clean car means that I'm an organized person. Even though, at some level, I know I'm really a disorganized person with a clean car. Still, I resolve to keep my car too clean and not worry that it's becoming a sexual fetish.

UnResolution Number Four. I love my two cats, Mimi and Vivi, and four dogs, Penny, Angie, Ruby The Unmedicated Corgi, and Little Tony The Anatomically Incorrect Cavalier. They make me happy every day. I love to walk them, talk to them, and kiss them on the lips. Well, this Christmas, I added to the brood, a little female Cavalier puppy named Peach.

And she's a peach.

I know it sounds crazy and weird but she's already making me happier, sleeping beside my laptop as I write.

With the TV on, showing *Analyze This*.

Happy New Year!

Happy New Year

~~~~~~~~

It's true that I believe in UnResolutions, that is, resolving to keep doing things you like. But I also try to make the old-fashioned, conventional New Year's resolutions.

As usual, I'm easy on myself.

I know I'm not going to keep all my resolutions, and that's okay with me.

I always resolve to do things I know I won't do, so why should New Year's be any different? Last week, I resolved to get my truck inspected and my roots done. I didn't do either. If you inspected my roots, I'd get a ticket.

Don't mistake me, it's not as if I didn't intend to do the things I'd resolved to do. It just didn't work out. And I don't feel guilty about it, because there are so many other things to feel guilty about.

Ask Mother Mary.

Maybe the problem is with the word *resolution*. It has a legal vibe that's no fun at all. A *resolution* is for a corporation or a national constitution. *Resolved* is a good start to a preamble about the right to free speech, but it's overkill for me losing five pounds.

Resolution is just too intense for what we're talking about. If you look it up in the thesaurus, its synonyms are *dauntlessness, staunchness,* and *tenacity.*

Got a headache yet?

I do.

I suggest we replace the word *resolution* with *wish,* and from now on, we can all make *wishes* for New Year's. It's dull to make a resolution, but it's fun to make a wish. It makes you think of birthday cake.

Everybody loves birthday cake.

And if you look up *wish* in the thesaurus, its synonyms are *desire, hankering,* and *itch.*

Isn't that better?

Wish doesn't take itself as seriously as *resolution,* and neither should we. We're just people, and often we fall short. To err is human, right? For *Homo sapiens,* failure is a job requirement.

If we stop *resolving* and start *wishing,* we would never fail, because nobody ever expects a wish to come true. For example, I wish I could marry George Clooney. I wish I could lose five pounds. I wish I had naturally blond hair, so I didn't have to worry about my roots in the first place.

We know that none of my *wishes* is going to come true. But I really do *wish* for them. And I'd like to keep *wishing* for them. *Wishing* fulfills a human need that goes beyond common sense. After all, we buy Powerball tickets and hold presidential elections.

Somebody wins, but it's never us.

I bet some of you are reading this and shaking your head. You agree that *resolution* is too hard-core, but you think *wish* is for slackers. You seek a compromise between *resolution* and *wish*. You wonder, isn't there a middle ground?

Don't despair. I have another word.

Aim.

How does *aim* suit you? You could make a list of New Year's *aims*. I view *aim* as *resolution* with a fallback. With *aim,* you get to announce your *resolution*, but it automatically includes a Plan B. Like an exit strategy, built-in.

How would *aim* work?

Let's say you aim to lose ten pounds this coming year. That's like saying you resolve to lose ten, but you'd settle for losing two. In other words, if you lose ten, great. If you lose five, also great. But if you lose only one, then you have to feel guilty and worthless for the holidays next year.

Aim is like a pre-nup. You want to keep your *aim*. You will try to keep your *aim*. In fact, you *aim* to keep your *aim*. But you're realistic enough to know that you might not be able to keep your *aim*. Because you can get so sick of your *aim*, it's not even funny. And if your *aim* tells that duck story one more time, you might commit murder.

But I'm off track. Bottom line, if you don't keep your *aim,* you keep the house, the Schwab account, and the car.

Aim is growing on me if you can't tell. *Aim* has the connotation of physically aiming at something, like a target, but there's wiggle room, in case your *aim* was off. As if you just missed the mark. Close, but no cigars. The failure wasn't your fault, exactly. The sun was in your eyes.

You with me?

Come along. I'm converting to *aim*. *Aim* works better for me.

Observe.

Here is my New Year's aim: I aim to marry George Clooney, but I would settle for sleeping with him.

Am I aiming too high?

Or would that be a miracle?

Love and Meatballs

By Francesca Scottoline Serritella

The relationship between a grandparent and grandchild is an easy one to take for granted. I was lucky enough to have my grandmother as my babysitter when my mom was working; she was like a second mother to me, so we've always been close. But time has passed, she moved to South Beach to live with my uncle, and I've grown and moved out of my mom's house, so you know how it goes. Things change.

Mainly, my grandmother got too cool for me.

Not that she loves me any less, I'm not sure my grandmother could love me any more. But the last time she stayed with us, I really wanted to spend quality time with her. I didn't merely want to be in the same room with her, I wanted to do things together, share things. But I had to face it.

She's just not that into me.

For example, I got up early every morning with my mom, so all three of us could have breakfast together. But we quickly discovered that my grandmother sleeps in until noon or later.

She's a hard-partying granny.

When she did shuffle downstairs, her short white hair disheveled, I offered to make eggs. But all she wanted for breakfast was an Apple Fritter from Dunkin' Donuts, and would I mind running out to pick one up for her?

So much for brunch.

But, hey, when you're eighty-six and you beat throat cancer, you're allowed to enjoy whatever fatty, sugary confection you want. I figured I couldn't expect her to change her routine, so I should try to show an interest in her hobbies.

Namely, "the puzzles."

My grandmother is a master of word puzzles: crosswords, cryptograms, acrostics, seek-and-finds, etc. She has whole books of them. But crosswords are her very favorite, her puzzle soulmate. Every morning, my mom would lay out the daily crossword from two different newspapers for her, and my grandmother did them first thing. They're practically part of her diet.

I was an English major in college, I'm a better than average Scrabble player, and my mind is young and sharp, so I thought maybe I could help her do one.

Turns out, I suck.

In retrospect, I was deluded to think I could possibly help the Grand Master with her puzzles. She's been honing her skill for more than a half century. She could probably teach Will Shortz a thing or two.

But I was worse than unhelpful. I was a handicap.

First, I answered the clues out of order, which made my grandmother insane. I had the gall to skip around, when the only proper way to go about a crossword puzzle is block by block.

Then, when she directed me to fill in an answer, I did so with a black pen. Outrage. Who raised me? Red is the only acceptable color ink. Black matches the lines and numbers, and therefore is not clear.

Red has contrast, not to mention style.

I let her do her puzzles in peace.

So I took a different tack. My grandmother was a hot number when she was younger, and one beauty habit she's kept over the years is filing her nails. Her fingernails are always shaped and smoothed to perfection. She carries an emery board with her at all times.

She refused to carry that Life Alert we got her, but God help her if she can't find her nail file.

Maybe it's genetic, because nails are sort of my secret talent. I can do a perfect, freehand French manicure, even on my right hand. Impressive, right? So I thought, perfect—I'll paint my grandmother's nails for her!

Not interested.

Nail polish chips in a day, not to mention contains dangerous chemicals, she says.

This from a woman who held a cigarette between her fingers for sixty-five years.

So a "no" to the nails.

Finally, I make her an offer she can't refuse.

"Will you teach me how to make your famous meatballs and sauce?"

This got her excited. She carefully dictated the shopping list, full of secret ingredients like onion powder, garlic powder, dried basil, and diced, pureed, and paste forms of canned tomato.

Freshness is against tradition.

When I returned from the store, I cleaned off the kitchen table and laid everything out for her approval. Everything passed inspection except one thing:

Me.

"You're wearing nail polish," she said.

"So?"

"You can't make the meatballs with nail polish on. It will poison them."

I knew better than to resist. "I'll take it off."

"With remover?" Her brown eyes got even larger behind her giant glasses. "Even worse. You can watch."

But I begged, I pleaded with her to let me make them, and no grandparent can resist a wailing grandchild, even if she's twenty-four.

So we set to work. I made plenty of rookie mistakes—making some too big, too small, too wet, or too dry—but even my grandmother's nitpicking was loving. "No, Kitten, like *this*," she would say.

If only this picture were scratch and sniff.

And when my over-enthusiasm for rolling sent a meatball flying through the air and onto the floor, she didn't scold me. She laughed.

She may pretend I'm a nuisance, but I am her favorite nuisance.

When we were finished, we had made the most delicious meatballs in existence. Over fifty of them, which should give you an idea of my family's portion control.

That night, the three of us had a spaghetti-and-meatballs feast. As I was clearing the table, I asked my grandmother if she could write out the recipe so I could make them on my own.

"My hands feel dirty. I'll do it tomorrow."

But her hands looked clean to me.

When I reminded her the next day, she said, "My eyes are tired. Later, Cookie."

We love each other like crazy, emphasis on "crazy."

But she did two puzzles after that.

What gives? At first I didn't understand why my grandmother was reluctant to write down the recipe. Then it occurred to me that maybe she didn't want me to make the meatballs without her. Not that she wanted to be the lone expert, but that she wanted to feel needed. She didn't gather from my interest in breakfast, puzzles, and manicures how much she already was.

When we were saying goodbye at the airport, my grandmother pointed a finger at me and said, "Don't think I forgot. I'll write the recipe when I get home and send it to you."

I gave her a hug. "We'll make them next time you come up."

Big Love

I'm in love.

With my big TV.

It's Big Love.

My big TV takes up the entire family room, but that's one of its many charms. True, we're in the early stages of our romance, when I still find its faults adorable. The minute it starts sucking its teeth, I'm outta here.

But I have a feeling this one's a keeper. For example, honesty is the most important element in any relationship, and my TV always tells the truth, especially in high definition. It shows me every wrinkle on every face—except mine. How many home appliances make you feel younger?

In fact, if my third husband will be a dog, my fourth will be a big TV.

And now I have the best of both, my new puppy Peach and a big TV. We watch football together while I write, with Peach and Little Tony sleeping on either side of me, flanking the laptop on my lap. At other times, they take over and kick the laptop off my lap. If I ruled the world, they'd permanently replace the laptop, but they don't pay the bills.

And by the way, I never forget about the other dogs, the two golden retrievers and Ruby The Corgi. The whole family has been known to sit on the couch together, watching the big TV during these long winter evenings, a motley lineup of fur and hair, sharing the same knitted blanket.

The cats, Mimi and Vivi, curl up in a nearby ottoman and the best chair in the house, respectively. They control the remote.

So it's inevitable that I'm watching the big TV with five dogs and two cats when a show comes on A&E about animal hoarding. I'd never heard of animal hoarding, and it comes as a surprise to me. Apparently, there are people who live alone with too many pets.

Awkward.

Back on the couch, we all exchange glances. Nobody says a word. The cats turn up the volume.

We watch the show in silence, and I try to spot the difference between me and the animal hoarder on the TV. I am relieved to find one basic difference.

He wears a baseball cap.

I don't.

Therefore, I'm not an animal hoarder. Also he said that his house was cluttered, but not dirty. I'm just the opposite. My house is dirty, but not cluttered. In my defense, it's hard not to have sagebrush of dog hair rolling across the carpet when you have pets, but this argument may be a little circular.

I remember a book club party I gave recently at my house, as a thank-you to book clubs who have the great judgment to read me. At the party, I gave a talk, after which I asked for questions. A hand went up immediately, and I called on an attractive woman.

"Yes, what's your question?"

"It's more like a comment," the woman answered. "I want to say that my book club loved your book, and we appreciate your having us to your home. And we love that you're so real and didn't clean for us."

Everybody exchanged glances. Nobody said a word. I wasn't sure how to answer, so I told the truth, since honesty is so integral to a relationship:

"Actually, I cleaned the house for two days before the party."

Laughter ensued, which is the point after all, but the question stuck with me. I realized that the problem was probably the way I kept the books I own, which number a thousand or so. I love to read and I buy a lot of books, and I kept all my books stacked everywhere in the dining room. They filled chairs, covered the dining room table, and blanketed the sideboard. There were even piles on the floor. I liked the look, but it made me think that maybe it wasn't such a great thing, so I recently got some bookshelves, separated the books by fiction and nonfiction, and shelved them in alphabetical order by author. Now I have my own personal library, all pretty and organized, and I know the truth.

I'm not an animal hoarder, I'm a book hoarder.

Do you know what they call people who hoard books?

Smart.

The First Lesson of the New Year

More home repair drama from which I learn a Valuable Life Lesson.

You may remember that for Christmas, I got my house a big TV. It's in the family room, where it doubles as a room divider, if not the Great Wall of China. The TV begins our saga, because it requires rewiring that sends an electrician down to my basement, and when he comes back upstairs, he asks:

"When was the last time anybody was in your crawlspace?"

Kind of personal, but I let it go. "Why?"

"It's raining down there."

These are words nobody wants to hear, especially on Christmas Eve, which is when our story takes place. I asked, "What happened?"

"The subfloor is soaked, the insulation's wet and falling off, and there's water all over. A pipe burst in your radiant heating."

At first I didn't even remember that I had radiant heating. Then I had a flashback from my second marriage, filled with enemy fire and assorted weaponry. I recalled that during the war, radiant heating had been installed in the entrance hall, but I had never used it. That it would explode and destroy Christmas Eve was somehow inevitable.

Anyway, the storm in the basement requires an emergency plumber, who goes down to the crawlspace and determines that I need an emergency HVAC guy, who arrives two hours later, just ahead of Santa. God bless the plumbers and HVAC guys, who work the same hours as mythical figures and don't get half the credit.

The HVAC guy turns off the shower in the crawlspace but tells me that the plumber has to come back, which doesn't happen until the afternoon of New Year's Eve, when he informs me that I have to call an emergency water-damage company or I could have a "microbial problem."

I stop him right there. "You mean, *mold*?"

"Yes," he answers, cringing, because now he has an hysterical homeowner on his hands. *Mold* is a word that terrifies me even more than *IRS audit* or *blind date*. Plus, no woman wants microbes in her crawlspace.

So I call the water-damage people, and they zoom over, rip out the soggy insulation, and install equipment in the basement, there to suck out the microbial water. The floor in the entrance hall is wet under the rug, so they install a major dehumidifier and an Injectidry system, which is a large black box from which emanates yellow tentacles covered with red spikes, like the sea creature that ate New Year's Eve.

They tape the tentacles to mats all over the kitchen, family room, and entrance hall, then switch on the machines, warn me they'd be loud, and leave. Five minutes later, loud doesn't begin to describe it. It sounds like a locomotive idling in the room, and as happy as I am that my moldy water is vanishing, I can't take the din. It scares the cats and dogs, especially new puppy Miss Peach, who huddles against me, shaking. I cuddle them all on the couch and turn on my superbig TV, but we can't hear the shows over the clamor.

By the way, in case you think this sounds like the most boring New Year's Eve ever, you should know that until the pipes burst, I had been looking forward to spending the evening reading and watching the big TV with my little pets. I am the ultimate homebody. Also couchbody, TVbody, and bookbody.

Anyway, to get to the life lesson part, I endured the locomotive noise until I couldn't stand it, then I got up and examined the dehumidifier and the scary Injectidry machine. I found the power switches, but I didn't know if I should turn off the machines. I was worried I'd damage them, and I didn't want to call the water-damage people and bother them further on New Year's Eve. Bottom line, I didn't know if I was allowed to turn

Happy New Year.

them off, so at midnight, the dogs, cats, and I watched the ball drop on mute and went miserably to bed.

But on the morning of the New Year, I awoke with a new determination. Last year, I was a woman who hesitated and suffered. But in the New Year, I was wiser and older, even if by a day.

Kind reader, I went downstairs and turned off the machines.

What did I learn?

Never ask permission.

Droopy Drawers

I had some excitement at the house the other night, when Daughter Francesca was home. I was getting ready to go to bed, and the cats and dogs were in their usual positions in my bedroom. Penny, Little Tony, Peach, and Ruby The Crazy Corgi were in my bed, and Mimi was curled into a black ball on the bedroom chair. Vivi was nowhere in sight, but then again, she rarely interrupts her skulking to make even a cameo appearance.

But Angie, the older golden retriever, was sitting and staring at my chest of drawers, which are built into the bedroom wall. The top drawers were partway open, with socks falling out, because I leave them that way. My drawers are a mess because I have better things to do.

"Look at that." Francesca frowned. "That's weird, what Angie's doing."

"Whatever." I was tired. I'm always tired when I go to bed. I feel sorry for people who can't sleep. I sleep for all of us. And when I want to go to bed, stay out of my way.

"She never does that."

"There's a first time for everything." I went over to the bed and shoveled some animals aside to clear a space for my weary bones. I have a king-size bed of which I occupy six inches, surrounded on all sides by fur, and I wouldn't have it any other way.

But Francesca was eyeing the drawers with concern. "Something's there," she said, and as if on cue, a weird scratching sound came from the chest of drawers.

Something was behind it. Only I didn't know there was room behind it, and I didn't know what could be behind it. Now I was awake. I got out of bed, slowly. "Maybe it's a mouse."

"Or a raccoon, or a squirrel."

"Or a dragon, or a psycho killer."

The dogs looked over, Ruby started barking, and suddenly, my socks came alive.

Francesca screamed, I screamed, and we started hugging each other, screaming while the dogs barked and barked, and my socks came spilling out of the drawer, followed by Vivi the cat, who merely yawned when she saw us hysterical.

I should have known, because of Angie.

Vivi and Angie are newly in love.

Vivi isn't affectionate to me, and doesn't even know me, but I keep trying to get her to love, plying her with overpriced cat food, an occasional saucer of milk, or leftover scrambled eggs. She gobbles up the food, but never looks at me in gratitude, and there's never a thank-you note. I'd resigned myself to the fact that she didn't like anybody in the house, except that now, out of nowhere, she has fallen in love with Angie.

Vivi spends all her time following Angie around as she goes through her day, from walking around the block, to sitting in a chair, and finally walking from her food dish to her water dish and back to her chair.

Sounds familiar.

When Angie lies down, Vivi curls up next to her, so they have trans-species spooning.

I regard that as proof that Vivi isn't sociopathic, because before Angie, her best friend was the kitchen faucet. She used to rub her face against the faucet, so I naturally assumed that she wanted the water turned on, maybe for a drink. I would turn on the faucet, but she would just get up and walk away. Then I thought it was because I was watching, so I would turn on the faucet and walk out of the kitchen. But the same thing happened.

Then I thought she was trying to scratch her chin on the faucet, so I tried to scratch her chin for her, in the same spot. And she got up and walked away. So now she spends her time staring at the kitchen faucet, occasionally rubbing against it, and maybe fantasizing about it, for all I know.

I don't understand Vivi at all.

You know what I mean, if you have any kind of pet. We come to know them, whatever little soul that's in there, and also the way they think. The test is that their actions can become predictable over time, and that's been true of all of my pets, all my life, except Vivi.

I don't understand why she squeezes behind drawers or why she loves her faucet and Angie.

Vivi remains a mystery, even to a mystery writer.

GNO

~~~~~~~~

I just went on a girls' night out, or a GNO, and it got me thinking. How did that term, and even its acronym, enter the vernacular?

Why do we specify when it's a girls' night out, as opposed to a boys' night out? And is it because a boys' night out is the norm, so we need to specify when it's a girls night out, which is, what, bizarre?

We all got dressed up for each other and even took pictures. Again, I doubt that guys dress up for a boys' night out, and they leave the flip cameras at home. When girls go out, it's not just dinner, it's prom.

By way of background, eight of us went out to a restaurant in NYC, hosted by my great friend Robin, who has an apartment in the city. She brought two of her friends, one of whom is single and one who isn't, and I joined them with Daughter Francesca and my assistant Laura, who's married.

I specify because we spent the first hour of our girls' night out talking about boys, and whether we have them or not. I'm betting that on a boys' night out, they talk about playoffs.

The second hour of the night we spent talking about how we never go out, why we have so much fun when we go out, how we should go out more, why do we need an excuse to go out, and isn't it crazy that it takes five weeks of planning for girls to go out? We couldn't even have the experience without talking incessantly about it while we were having it.

Which is when I realized that the Heisenberg principle is completely wrong.

As you may know, the Heisenberg principle holds that an experience is necessarily altered by its being observed, but I disagree. Heisenberg never went on a GNO, and his principle doesn't apply when the people having the experience are the ones observing it, and they're still talking about it as they have it, all at the same time. For girls, the talk *is* the experience, especially when margaritas are present.

Mine was pineapple.

Which could have been a mistake.

I asked for a pineapple margarita as soon as I sat down, not because I'm a practiced drunk but because I'd been looking forward to it for two weeks, which gives you an idea of my social life. I wanted the pineapple margarita because I remembered that I'd had a terrific one once with Francesca. But the waiter looked at me funny and said they'd try to make me one, and she reminded me that it was a pineapple martini that I'd had that time and there might not be such a thing as a pineapple margarita.

Oh.

This mattered not at all by the third pineapple margarita, which tasted great because it was yellow.

And whether it was because of the alcohol or the estrogen, what happened then was that we girls'-night-outers got to laughing a little loud.

Or rather, one of us did.

Me.

Some men at the bar turned around at the noise, but my back was to them, so I didn't see. I bet they were turning around to look at Robin, who is drop-dead gorgeous, but she's so modest that she assumed it was because of our (read, my) loudness, and she said:

"Sorry, we're celebrating." Then Robin pointed at me. "She's getting married."

Wha?

Huh?

Me?

This sent all of us into new gales of laughter, and I thought it was so funny, but then I wondered:

Why do I need a reason to be loud?

Men don't need a reason to be loud.

Girls should have an equal right to bad manners.

And I wasn't loud anyway.

The pineapple margaritas were loud, not me.

They don't get out enough.

They need an MNO, poor things.

Designing Woman

By Francesca Scottoline Serritella

I've always looked forward to decorating my own place. When my mother and stepfather parted ways, my mom conducted a massive home makeover. Gone was the compromised style of a marriage; here was the décor rebellion of a divorcée. She painted the all-white kitchen orange, reupholstered the red tartan sofa in a golden honeycomb, and covered the walls with rainbow Peter Max paintings. When she was finished, the house was sunny, feminine, and a little crazy—in other words, it was *her*.

As much as I love her, I was excited to live in a place that was me.

However, decorating your first apartment is not as easy as I thought it would be.

First problem: my taste is better than my budget. I envisioned a plush couch with a funky mismatched ottoman. A shop down the street has the most adorable vintage glass chandeliers that'd be great over my table. And a giant, floor-length mirror would really open up the narrow entrance hall.

All good ideas, stylish even.

But my wallet is less Crate & Barrel, more Craigslist. And sadly, IKEA does not have much by way of vintage glass chandeliers.

No use crying over financial realities. I've found ways around pesky money problems. No, I am not advocating theft or credit-card debt. I turned to something arguably more dangerous:

eBay.

I figured eBay could be the way to get unique decorative pieces on the cheap. What could go wrong?

First, there were the little piggy salt and pepper shakers. They looked so cute in the pictures, a little boy pig and a little girl one, hand-painted, and authentic! Authentic what, I wasn't sure. But they were $3.99 and the auction was going to end in two minutes! So I leapt into action and—sold! For $3.99.

I was the only bidder.

Maybe because, as became clear when they arrived, each was less than an inch and a half long.

They were salt and pepper thimbles.

Shipping was three times the original price, so it wasn't as cost-effective as I had hoped, and, considering that I had selected this particular set from a list of over five hundred, not particularly time-effective either.

Okay, so now I try to get my hands on something before I buy it.

But this hands-on approach took on an all-too-literal meaning when I realized that most of the furniture I could afford carried this ominous warning:

"Assembly required."

Or its more treacherous cousin, "some assembly required."

"Some assembly required" translates in English to: just as much assembly required, now with fewer directions.

Fine, no problem. I got out my tool-kit-for-chicks (pink-handled tools, a gift from Mom), put on a Talking Heads playlist (because I was raised right), pulled on my Converse sneaks, and tied a bandana around my head.

Manual labor is better when you accessorize.

Turns out, building furniture was fun!

For the first thirty minutes.

For the next several hours, I had only my feminist self-righteousness to keep me going. But keep me going it did, and I accepted this effort as a rite of passage for being young and on your own.

The MVP of any city dweller's tool kit is, without a doubt, the measuring tape. All of these apartments are an amalgam of tiny, weird spaces—a skinny alley of a galley kitchen, or a sleeping "nook," meaning "closet."

Design gurus love to tell you to use dual-functioning furniture to save space, like it's the easiest thing in the world. And initially, I was with them. My ottoman is essentially an upholstered box that can hold blankets, and if you flip the top to the hard surface side, it doubles as a small coffee table.

Yes, I felt very clever when I bought it.

But storing my decorative throw blanket wasn't my main space problem. I still have a kitchen with no shelves. I still have a bedroom that can't fit a dresser. And while I'm trying to be innovative, I'm starting to resent those dopey ideas for multi-purpose living.

No, I do not want my oven to double as a pantry. Nah, I don't think my dog's metal crate makes for an "industrial" end table. No, I don't think a bookshelf becomes a "secretary" desk simply by putting a stool in front of it.

I'd rather have no room to walk than sit on a barstool with my feet on the paperbacks.

There are so many decisions that go into decorating your first place. Recently, I decided to buy bookshelves. I found the perfect ones, just narrow and shallow enough to fit in my bedroom and still leave room for me to get in and out of bed. They were just what I'd been looking for. There was only one thing left to decide:

What color?

The options were white or pink. But it's not a soft pink. It's a juicy, watermelon pink, a sunset-over-South-Beach pink—and lacquered, no less! A little much, perhaps. White, on the other hand, is classic. White shelves are versatile, at home in the kitchen or in the bedroom. White would match my bed frame. Nothing in my apartment is pink.

It's kind of a no-brainer.

They're delivering my flamingo pink bookshelves next week.

The joy of living on my own is I have only myself to please, and I like pink. It makes me happy.

Did you forget I was raised in an orange kitchen?

Take Your Medicine

~~~~~~~

I'm trying to remember when food became medicine.

Because everybody knows that food is love.

And comfort.

And a reward.

The idea that food is medicine might have started with all this talk about antioxidants, which evidently aren't things that prevent rust, but things you have to eat every day, like a magic pill that wards off all manner of dreaded diseases. Then I started hearing about free radicals, which was another thing to be avoided, although to a person of a certain age, a free radical is Abbie Hoffman or Jerry Rubin.

Young people will have to look up these references. I suggest the *World Book Encyclopedia,* now housed under glass at the Smithsonian.

Bring a quill.

Anyway, I wanted to learn about antioxidants and free radicals, because I don't want to die or get rusty, so I bought a book about superfoods, which explained that blueberries and beans were better for you than potato chips and popcorn.

Who knew?

I studied the book, which says that you should try to eat the superfoods every day, like more magic pills, and it listed the good things in each superfood.

Or maybe the super things.

For example, I learned that blueberries have magnesium, turkey has zinc, oats have manganese, wild salmon has selenium, walnuts have arginine, and tomatoes have chromium.

Wow!

I would have thought that only cars had chromium.

And batteries had selenium.

And magnesium is something in an Etch A Sketch.

And zinc is something you smear on your nose to prevent sunburn.

I've never even heard of arginine, which clearly belongs on the periodic table, under the chemical symbol TaStes TeRriBle.

So now when I plan a meal, I don't think about what tastes good or what I feel like eating. I ignore all my cravings and all the dishes that make me feel happy. No food in a TV commercial tempts me, because it's guaranteed that nothing in Kentucky Fried Chicken has chromium. Instead I select dosages of superfoods and rotate them around for a week of supermeals.

Super?

Which brings me to quinoa.

A friend of mine was raving to me recently about quinoa, saying how good it is for you and how much protein and fiber it has, so I went immediately to the store to get some. I couldn't find any because I was looking for something spelled like "keenwa," and all they had was something clearly pronounced like "quinn-noah." The salesperson told me that quinn-noah was really keen-wa, and who am I to complain, because try spelling Scottoline.

Plus I'm getting the idea that if you can't pronounce it, it definitely has antioxidants, and none of its radicals will be free.

Free Angela.

Again, look it up.

So I take home the box of quinoa, boil it up, and dump it onto a plate, where it mounds like snow. And not white, new-fallen snow, but second-day snow, after the plow has gone by, shoving it up against your car.

Yummy.

It tastes like nothing, or maybe it tastes like antioxidants, or maybe just like rust. I dress it up with sautéed tomatoes, which ward off diseases. And garlic, which wards off a sex life.

So far, so good.

And I told myself that it didn't matter if I didn't like the quinoa, because I'm not allowed to like my food anymore anyway, and in time I got a cookbook all about quinoa, which taught me that it was some kind of grain, discovered by an American guy who went to Bolivia, because then it grew only in the Andes.

Which I thought was a mint, but back to the story.

And although the American guy brought quinoa seeds back to the United States to try to grow them in Colorado, he still imports the seeds from Bolivia because we had the correct altitude but not the correct latitude. Then I realized that I didn't have the correct attitude.

I want to be open to new foods, even ones that double as medicine.

So I tried to change the way I think about antioxidants and free radicals.

And I sprayed a little lemon on the quinoa, and it wasn't so bad.

For old snow.

Adults Only

One of the oddest experiences you may ever have is visiting your adult child for the first time. And while we're on the subject, "adult child" is one of the oddest phrases ever.

I'm not sure it even makes sense.

I guess that, at age 24, Daughter Francesca is considered an adult child, and God knows I've met a child adult in my time.

But to stay on point, Francesca has lived in New York for a year now, and I still feel weird when I visit her. It's different from when I saw her at college, because though she was living on her own there, she was in a dorm and therefore hadn't become an official adult child. But now that she has an apartment and a lease, there's no question.

So when do I stop calling her an adult child and start calling her an adult?

If you're a mother, the answer is easy:

Never.

I think it's hard to let go of your child, whether she's going to college or kindergarten, whether she's walking down the aisle or backpacking in France. And if having your kid move out is bad enough in theory, visiting her makes it real.

Can I just say that I'm not completely on board with this whole moving-away part?

I think it's something we don't talk about, for fear of being labeled insanely overprotective.

Like that's a bad thing?

Honestly, I keep it to myself, but every time I visit her, I see for myself how treacherous her life can be. A woman from her building was mugged and her jaw was broken. Another woman she knows was hit by a van as she crossed the street, her nose broken.

A face is in jeopardy in the big city.

Francesca lives in a nice neighborhood, and when I walk around, I see lots of nice people, but I also see drunks and drug addicts. True, I don't have proof of their occupation, but they wear black-leather jackets and have lots of tattoos and piercings.

So they could be lawyers.

But in my defense, there was a time once when a drunk/drug addict staggered into a pet store where we were, tried to kiss Francesca, then fell crying on the floor. She felt sorry for him, and I wanted him dead.

Keep your lips off my baby.

And my thoughts ran wild. What if he had a knife? A gun?

When I walk down her street, I worry, is this where she walks every day? And where can I buy a large plastic bubble?

It only gets weirder when I cross the threshold into her apartment, where she asks me to sit down and offers me coffee and a sandwich.

Who raised this child?

It's sweet of her to offer, but it's for me to sit her down and make her a sandwich. I can't shake a habit of twenty years so easily. My job is to feed and water. So we bump into each other as we both go for the sandwich plate.

She wins.

And as proud of her as I am, and I am so proud, I do wish I could help her just a little. I wasn't aware of this until my last visit, when I found myself cleaning up her apartment while we talked, even though it was already neat and clean. I started picking up a stray newspaper here and there, and she finally waved me onto the couch.

"You don't have to do that," she said, softly. "Please, stop."

"But I can help."

"Let's just talk instead."

Still I wanted a vacuum cleaner. I could hardly wrap my mind around the role reversal. My world was going topsy-turvy, but I sat down and we started talking and the chores were forgotten among the chatter.

We're making a new way to be together, visit by visit.

The hardest part comes when I have to leave, and again, on the last visit, I was supposed to go on Sunday night after dinner, but I found myself making excuses to stay over. When it started raining, I decided it was dangerous to drive home.

(In truth, I drive in blizzards.)

Also I noted that *Big Love* was on TV, and I love *Big Love*.

(But I had set the DVR before I left home.)

Plus Monday was a holiday, so the traffic would be less if I stayed over and drove home the next day.

(There's no traffic at ten o'clock at night anyway.)

So of course I weaseled my way into staying over, but I

couldn't stop there. I insisted that she let me drive her to the dry cleaner with her dirty clothes, then I offered to run errands with her in the car, then we could have lunch.

She looked over at me, in the front seat.

She said I was being nice.

But I wasn't.

I was being a mother.

And she's an adult.

Cat and Mouse

You know I have way too many dogs, which constitute the sum total of my social life. But the pet who takes up most of my time is a cat.

Vivi.

You may remember that I live with two cats, Mimi and Vivi. Mimi is nice, and Vivi is mean. Mimi is affectionate, and Vivi is nasty. Mimi is good, and Vivi is evil. In other words, Mimi is Gallant, and Vivi is John Wayne Gacy.

And she's up to some new tricks.

She's accelerated her occasional mouse murder to a killing spree. I know that many people don't let their cats out at all, but I have plenty of room and live near a wooded area, so both cats go out in the day and come in at night. Which means that every morning, my first chore is cleaning up mouse remains.

Wake up and smell the tails.

I won't get too graphic, but it's not pretty. Vivi doesn't merely kill mice, she dismembers them. If I wanted to, I could reassemble the body parts and put together a grotesque mouse puzzle. It's not like she eats them, either, because she's always ravenous when she comes in. I stuff her with high-rent cat food so she'll stop the killing. Her latest culinary temptation is Tender Tongol Tuna, which Fancy Feast calls "Appetizers for Cats."

Maybe that's the problem, it's just an appetizer?

But that's not the problem. Vivi gets dry food, too, and table scraps.

Bottom line, she kills for fun.

I'm no forensics expert, but I've figured out her MO. She kills the poor thing, takes it apart, and arrays its tail, legs, and ears around the back patio, so they spell POINT OF NO RETURN.

Or YE SHALL NOT PASS.

And IF DOGS ARE SO GREAT, WHY CAN'T THEY DO THIS?

Every morning, I spend half an hour picking up all this disgusting debris, then fetch some hot water and wash blood off my patio.

It ain't *House & Garden* around here.

And it gets worse. Now what's happening is that when I call her to come in at night, I catch her in the act of chasing, stalking, or trying to demolish some terrified fieldmouse, and I have to save the mouse.

I saved three mice last month.

Yay?

I know. It's counter-intuitive, which is a euphemism for dumb. I don't really want mice around my house, where they could get inside, so when I catch Vivi in the act, I should just go back to the family room, turn on the TV, and crank up the volume, so I can't hear the cries for help.

I should mind my own business and pretend I didn't see anything, like a witness at a Gotti trial.

As we used to say, I don't want to get involved.

But I have to.

I'll be a coroner, but I won't be an accomplice.

So last night, I spent an hour in frigid weather, with a coat over my bathrobe, trying to save a mouse that I want dead.

Vivi had it cornered against the house, so I tried to rescue it by calling her frantically, but she ignored me. I picked up a stick and waved it around to distract her, with the dogs in the house, barking frantically. She ignored them the way she ignores me.

Vivi doesn't do frantic.

Then I ran into the house and got the Tongol Tuna, but I didn't have time to wrestle with the plastic top because she was

Homicidal Vivi.

closing in on the mouse, so I charged her, acting like I was go-ing to hurt her, which I never would, and the mouse saw its opening, darted across the patio, and scooted out of reach onto the porch furniture, and stopped to catch its breath on the back of a wrought-iron chair.

Victory?

Then I chased Vivi around the yard, while I ripped off the top off the tuna, and finally used it to lure her inside.

The mouse remained panting on the patio chair, then ran off into the night, undoubtedly to return to my house, bring-ing ticks and bubonic plague.

But before it left, I took its picture.

It's giving the thumbs up.

Batman and Robin

～～～～～

I just got off the phone with Mother Mary and I don't understand anything we said. It seems impossible that we communicate so badly, and I can't blame it on the cell phone, bad reception, or a faulty connection.

The faulty connection comes with the family.

We talked for about fifteen minutes, both of us speaking English, which is our first language. But it was as if we were having two different conversations. And I can't figure out when we took a wrong turn to Conversational Crazytown.

It started innocently enough, with me calling her to say hello, to which she replied, angrily:

"This cat is so spoiled!"

"Really, why?" I asked, surprised.

To interject some background, I've never heard Mother Mary get angry at the cat. At the dogs, yes. At my brother, yes. At the cable company, yes, and the humidity, yes, and the double-parking on their street, yes. Also at the City of Miami, yes, and all politicians, whom she regards as crooks and drunks, yes yes yes. She wakes up angry, then spends the day accumulating reasons therefor.

Retirement, Scottoline-style.

Andy Rooney is a piker compared with Mother Mary. He's merely cranky, which is kid stuff. In our dotage, we don't do curmudgeonly. The Flying Scottolines aim higher, for generalized hostility.

Many people take up a hobby in their golden years. Our hobby is aggravation.

Can't wait.

But Mother Mary never gets angry about the cat. She and my brother, whom you may recall live together in South Beach, love their cat, a skinny Siamese who's sixteen years old, named Putty Tat. In their defense, they didn't pick the cat's name. We're crazy, not stupid.

"She peed on your brother's bed!" my mother was saying.

"Uh-oh. When did she do this?"

"All the time!"

"Really? When did it start?"

"A year ago."

"*What?* Why didn't you do anything about it?"

"She does it on purpose."

So I'm thinking, what difference does that make, and why are you so mad about it now, but I didn't say anything for fear that her head would explode. And I was already figuring that the cat is sixteen, which is probably 3,000 in cat years, and nobody can vouch for their bladder after their 200th birthday. I got my own problems and I'm only 54, if you follow.

So I said, "Mom, maybe you should take her to the vet."

"She's so spoiled. I make her shrimp and I have to boil it. She won't eat the canned. And now your brother came home with a bedspread! I can't sleep a wink!"

I tried to follow. It was like a string of non sequiturs,

connected by changing tenses. "Ma, slow down. What does the shrimp have to do with the bedspread?"

"There's bats everywhere!"

"In the *house*?"

"Don't be fresh!" she snaps, even more exasperated, but I'm not being fresh, I'm being confused.

"Ma, where are the bats?"

"On the bed! There's like a thousand. They keep me awake!"

"Bats? Real bats?"

"He makes bat noises! It's not funny!"

On the phone, I hear my brother call out, "Batman and Robin!"

To interject again, my brother shouts in the background on most of our phone calls, and for that I'm grateful. I love him, and he's like my personal translator, fluent in Mary Scottoline. But I'm still confused. Also please note that nobody in my family ever explains anything. You have to cross-examine them, then piece the story together yourself. I'm trained as a lawyer, and this is difficult even for me.

"Ma, what about Batman and Robin?"

"How am I supposed to sleep with bats?"

My brother calls out, "I got her a Batman and Robin bed-spread! It came with a coloring book!"

I can't believe I'm hearing this right. She's eighty-six. "Ma, why did he get you that?"

"It has bats on one side, all bats! For him, he got one with trucks and cars!"

My brother calls out, "They were on sale at Ross!"

My mother calls back, "I can't sleep with bats!"

He shouts to her, "So turn it to the Batman side!"

She shouts back, "And have Batman lying on top of me?"

Okay, so this is about where I check out of the conversation. The picture of Mother Mary in bed with Batman burns itself into my imagination, and my mother and brother are off and running anyway. At some point, I suggest they take the cat to the vet and the bedspread back to Ross.

I don't know what they did with the coloring book.

Crash

By Francesca Scottoline Serritella

It all happened so fast. One moment everything was normal, and then, black. Then, white. Then, a blinking folder icon with a question mark inside it. And then, I knew.

My computer crashed.

I sat, frozen as the cursor on the screen. I came out of my catatonia after a few minutes, but my laptop remained non-responsive. I managed to access the Web on my cell phone and Google a description of my problem, but what I found was not good. Words like: "Hard drive failure!" "Ah, you got the question folder of death!" "Looks like your Mac is on its way to the big Apple store in the sky."

I felt my gorge rise. I was near hyperventilating. I thought I might cry. There was only one logical thing to do.

I called Mom.

"Are you okay?" she answered, alarmed. It didn't occur to me until then that it was after two in the morning.

"I'm fine, but omigod—"

"Are you hurt? Where are you?"

"Mom, I'm fine, I'm home."

"Did something happen to the dog?"

"No! Listen." I paused to find the strength. "My computer just crashed."

I heard my mom give her trademark irritated huff. "Honey, go to sleep. We'll deal with it in the morning."

"Wait! Did you hear me? I really think it's dead."

"Tomorrow, we'll talk tomorrow. Now come on, go back to sleep. Goodnight." *Click.*

I was so frustrated with my mother at that moment, but once calm, I had to recognize that the generation gap was to blame for her lack of sympathy. My mom uses her computer for work, email, shopping for books online, and Googling images of puppies.

I have my entire life on my computer. Every photo from the last six years, thousands of music files, all of my notes and schoolwork from college, my household budget, my datebook, my address book, my everything.

So I began the Odyssey of the twenty-first century:

Self-discovery via data-recovery.

First, I called the Apple store, and they told me the only "Genius" appointment available was at the uptown store at 4:20 P.M. Going to the Apple flagship store on a Sunday afternoon is the retail equivalent of telling someone you'll meet them in Times Square on New Year's Eve.

I stood on my tippy-toes to peer above the heads and spotted the glowing screen that read "Genius Bar," the North Star for all desperate Mac users.

I popped out from the tightly packed crowd like a watermelon seed between two fingers and threw myself prostrate before my appointed Genius. He took my laptop with hipster apathy.

As he was opening my computer, hooking it to various wires of life support, he asked, "So what happened when it crashed?"

"I was just using the Internet. I didn't drop it or anything. All of a sudden, it froze."

"What were you doing right before it froze?"

I hung my head. I would have to confess my sins. I was doing something online that is so shameful, so embarrassing, I could hardly say it. I was brought up better than this. I thought no one would know, I was in the privacy of my own home, but now—busted. I told him:

"I was putting my name into the *Jersey Shore* nickname generator."

You thought it was porn, right? No, worse. I was unmasked as a reality TV junkie. I once used that same laptop for my Harvard thesis.

My computer didn't crash, it quit.

So I waited while he typed at superhuman speed, plugged and unplugged, booted and rebooted. No more than a few minutes had passed when he looked up and said, "Okay, I think we're done."

My heart swelled. "Did you fix it?"

"No. Your hard drive failed. It's dead. Can't get anything off it."

"Nothing?"

"Nope."

"But how could this happen? I didn't drop it or do anything to it." My eyes welled with tears, which elicited a look of concern, or maybe fear.

"It's not your fault. Someday or another, all hard drives die.

Some just days out of the box, some years. There's not always a reason. Just like with people."

I couldn't point out the illogicality of this statement. I was too busy weeping.

"Um, don't cry." Twentysomething guys hate when girls cry. "Do you back up?"

For the record: if someone tells you, through tears, that their computer crashed, do not ask them, "Do you back up?" Not helpful.

"I back up my work files, but not any of my personal stuff."

"Maybe that should be the other way around."

Whoa. Deep.

It was the first Genius thing he'd said all day.

It reminded me of my mom's first two questions on the phone. I couldn't see it then, but she had the priorities straight. I am okay, the people and animals I love are okay. The lost files I miss the most are photos of those same people and animals: Pip's puppy pictures, my grandmother at my graduation, my road trip with my college roommates. But my old roommate is coming to visit, I just spoke with my grandmother, and Pip is curled in my lap.

The data may be lost, but I have the hard copies.

The Joy of Cookbooks

Okay, here's a weird thing I do. I hope you do it, too, because then we can understand why we do it, together. If not, I'm going to look really dumb.

But here goes:

I buy cookbooks. I read cookbooks. I love cookbooks. But I never cook anything from cookbooks.

And it's not like I don't cook. I cook all the time. I cook every night. Sometimes I even cook at lunch, either whole-wheat pasta with sautéed tomatoes and garlic, or grilled salmon with steamed spinach and garlic.

Impressed? Me, too. But I never use a cookbook.

Also now you know why I'm single.

And why I never worry about vampires.

We've already established that I hoard books, but I've never thought of myself as a cookbook hoarder. I buy plenty of cookbooks and receive more as gifts. I also get some free, like the great Costco cookbook, and others are sent to me from publishers, I guess for promotional purposes. I'm delighted by each one and I happily read them all, page by page. I savor the gorgeous photos of glossy cherry tarts, hearty potato casseroles, or moist chocolate layer cakes. I imagine all the delicious tastes, like the tang of a Meyer lemon, the sweetness of a candied pear, and the wiggly vein of cinnamon in a bread pudding.

But I never make any of them.

I clip recipes from magazines and newspapers, all the time. I even have a thick file folder for my clipped recipes, which I keep next to my cookbooks in the kitchen. I was so happy when *People* magazine started having recipes, and I clipped its simple recipe for Vanilla Cake. I cut out the Potato-Leek Gratin recipe from the Williams-Sonoma catalog. I couldn't believe my good luck when I found the recipe for Commissary Carrot Cake in the newspaper.

Yum.

I loved that carrot cake from The Commissary, back in the eighties. It was a great restaurant and a great dessert.

I'd love to taste that carrot cake again.

But I guarantee I won't make it from the recipe.

I even ripped out of a magazine in my dentist's office the recipe for Olive-Oil Poached Halibut with Brussels Sprouts and Mushrooms.

Sound good?

I thought so.

Am I going to make it?

Don't hold your breath.

Numbers don't lie, and put simply, I own twenty-three cookbooks, and in my whole entire lifetime, I have only cooked from a recipe on five occasions. And three of them were on Thanksgiving, when I checked *The Joy of Cooking* to remind me of how long to cook the turkey. By the way, the answer is always the same: Longer than I thought. From now on, I'm putting the turkey in at dawn.

The biggest enigma is the restaurant cookbook. This happens when I go to a fancy restaurant in New York, almost always taken there on business, when somebody else is paying. I've eaten at Union Square Café, Babbo, and Le Bernadin.

Wow. Delish. Life is good.

The food is so terrific that on the way out, I give in to temptation and buy the cookbook written by the celebrity chef. My reasoning is always, Wouldn't it be great if I could make Seared Scallop Salad With Spring Vegetables, just like Eric Ripert?

I can. In theory.

All I have to do is turn to pages 82–83 and get busy. The dish would be finished sooner than you can say *haricots verts*. You can't acquire the talent by acquiring the cookbook, but you don't need to. If you just follow the six easy steps, it all comes out in the same place.

Cooking is behavioral.

Or is it?

We'll never know.

In the end, my restaurant cookbooks morph into culinary souvenirs, though I do pull them off the shelf from time to time and salivate over the pictures.

Pornography for girls.

So maybe we can all figure out why we do this thing we do.

It's food for thought.

Or maybe thought for food.

Peachness

~~~~~~~~

I haven't written much about my new puppy Peach yet, because I've been avoiding the subject.

Not that I don't love her, because I do. In fact, no disrespect, but she might even be the best puppy I've ever had.

I'm avoiding the subject because anything written about her should begin with why I got her in the first place, and the answer is a simple, if unsatisfactory, one:

I don't know why.

This reveals something about me that I hadn't realized before, and wasn't especially proud of, until now.

When I understood that this is The Tao of Peach.

Let me explain.

We know I already had four dogs, which is three more dogs than anybody needs. The two golden retrievers are older, from an era when Daughter Francesca was around to play with them, and the two younger dogs, Ruby The Crazy Corgi and Little Tony, are empty-nest babies, meant to replace my daughter, though breast-feeding has been less than successful.

So, obviously, the last thing I needed was another empty-nest dog.

I already had one for each breast.

And I wish I could tell you that Peach is a rescue dog, but she isn't. Please know that I have had rescue dogs in my time, and so my rescue karma is excellent. Plus I contribute mightily to rescue organizations to absolve my guilt.

So how did Peach come into being?

It's not logical.

Bottom line, I was so crazy about Little Tony, who's a Cavalier King Charles Spaniel, that I wanted another Cavalier.

I told this to a fellow Cavalier fan, and she said, "Of course you want another one. They're like potato chips."

And though I appreciate the sentiment, and I love potato chips, that wasn't the reason. After all, I've had three golden retrievers in my time, too, and what are they?

Fritos?

It doesn't stand to reason.

And why is it that we always look to carbs for comparison, anyway? I'd go with candy. Have you ever had a single M&M? It can't be done.

Anyway, I tried to understand why your love for one dog makes you want another one. As a matter of logic, if you love your dog, you should probably just spend more time with him, but I already spend all my time with all my dogs, working at home, walking them, throwing them Kong balls, and taking them with me on trips for drive-thru coffee. In fact, I have been known to take four dogs to the local Dunkin' Donuts.

Little Tony gets munchkins, because he is one.

I was wondering if the doggie decision was like children. I had only one child and didn't think about wanting another, because I was fresh out of husbands. But I was guessing that normal people, who remain happily married, have a kid they love and decide that because they love it so much, they want another of its . . . breed.

Right?

Whatever, still not the reason.

To stay on point, I heard that a female Cavalier puppy was available, and I thought about it for a long time. It wasn't even an impulsive decision. I took two months to think about it, consulting Francesca and my friends, Franca and Laura, who were fine with whatever I decided. Together we ran through the factors and arguments, all of which proved that there was no reason to get another puppy.

Then I got in the car and picked up Peach.

Peach, Lisa's writing partner.

And never looked in the rear-view mirror, parentally speaking. She's got melty brown eyes, floppy ears, and a little russet-and-white body. She's calm, friendly, and a champion snuggler. She's housebroken and learned to sit in two days. She's tough enough to play with the big goldens and sweet enough to captivate Little Tony. He fell in love with her at first sight and made her his child bride, Mrs. Little Tony.

Ruby wishes her dead, of course.

Peach was the best decision I ever made, because now that I think of it, I did have a reason to get her, and it's simple:

I wanted to.

And nobody was around to stop me.

So maybe that's what she teaches.

Do what you want to.

Even if it looks a little wacky to the people at Dunkin' Donuts.

I Don't

By Francesca Scottoline Serritella

I'm not even twenty-five, and I've spotted my first sign of aging. It's nothing physical, not a wrinkle or a gray hair. I noticed it while reading a newspaper article on my tiny Black-Berry screen, though it has nothing to do with fading eyesight. I caught myself doing something that I'd never have done a year ago, something undeniably postgraduate, something, almost, *old*.

I was reading the Weddings section of the paper.

Gone are my days as a carefree college coed; now I'm in my freshman year of spinsterhood. When it comes to reading the wedding announcements, I have adopted the single-gal clichés I thought existed only in Cathy cartoons. Here's my confession, in writing.

I scour for the ages of the brides. This is the habit that shames me the most, since I consider myself a modern woman, forging my own path, free from the trappings of time and tradition. I lift weights at the gym, I alone built my IKEA furniture, and when I saw a mouse in my apartment, I trapped and disposed of it with minimal crying. Yet here I am, subtracting my age from all the brides'—twenty-eight, okay, I got four years to find the guy; thirty-three, cool, I can date a couple duds and focus on work; twenty-five, omigod I'd have to know him NOW.

Did I read too much Jane Austen in college? Or not enough? Is my dowry approaching recession as I get closer to the other side of twenty-five? My mom can throw in a couple chickens, if that will sweeten the deal, and a corgi too, although that won't sweeten anything.

And I read only the announcements with an accompanying photo. Why? Let's be honest, this is about superficial judgment and self-comparison. If I can't see the couple, how will I know who got the better end of the deal—did a chubby hubby luck out with a bombshell (he must be funny), or did Plain Jane nab a total hunk (girlfriend, tell me your secret)?

My newfound love of wedding photos extends beyond the Sunday paper. I am also a creeper of Facebook wedding albums. I friended an old classmate I barely knew, just to see her wedding photos. But I had to do it, because she always had the best clothes at school, so I knew her dress would be to die for, and she's beautiful and skinny as a rail, and *God*—I was in wedding-pic heaven.

Until, of course, I was in self-criticism hell.

But that's the drama of the Weddings section. It's a thrilling roller-coaster ride of self-esteem.

I've even upgraded my methods of voyeurism from photos to online videos of the couples. This is where it gets juicy. Occasionally, the story of the pair's serendipitous meeting or their gratitude for having found each other is lovely and moving, I sit smiling at the computer screen.

But other times, I cringe as red flags spring up like some cynical pop-up video: one bride whines that he took forever to propose; a groom bitterly recalls how she mocked his outfit on the first date; a dreamy-eyed couple shared love at first sight, although at the time, they were each married to other people. Good luck, kids!

Thing is, I don't even want to be married. Well, not yet. I think I just want to be marriageable. Some men have the misconception that women are desperate for a husband, but really, all we want is the knowledge that we're lovable. Doesn't everybody want that reassurance from time to time? Or maybe just on Sundays?

I took my new reading habits as a sign of my advancing age, but having confessed my sins, I feel pretty childish. I'm not ready to be married. I will be someday, when I've stopped comparing my age, my looks, my style, myself to any stranger smiling from the newspaper. I'll be ready when I can stop asking, "Am I lovable? Who loves me?" because I know the answer.

I do.

Deadhead

~~~~~~~~

Of course I read the obituaries.

I can't be the only one.

I do it every morning, in two newspapers, before I start to work. It takes a lot of time. I know, it sounds like stalling, but it's more like praying.

You'll see what I mean.

And it's not as if I started reading them recently, now that it's likelier I'll die than find a date.

In truth, I've read obits all my life, even as a kid.

I never saw them as being about deaths. I saw them as being about people, and I love people.

In other words, it's not a death story. It's a life story.

I'm always struck by how accomplished people are, and what they've done in their lives that's benefited me, only I didn't know it. For example, today I read an obit of a doctor who was one of the first to link smoking to cancer. I owe that guy, though I never knew him. I nagged my father to quit, and he did. I nagged Mother Mary to quit, but she didn't until she got and survived throat cancer.

Did I mention she's stubborn?

I read another obit, of a real estate developer who changed

the skyline of my beloved hometown, Philadelphia, and was also responsible for one of my favorite works of art, the giant *Clothespin* by Claes Oldenburg, which sits in front of the office building where I used to work.

I owe that guy, too.

I used to love to look out of my office window at that sculpture. It's a brown clothespin that's ten stories tall, and it made me smile, every day. Because of it, I bought a book about Claes Oldenburg and learned about his life and his art. So the least I can do is take the time to read about the man who introduced me to Claes Oldenburg and send him a mental thank-you note.

I always read the obits of soldiers. I owe it to them, each and every one of them. They're so young, and they're out there day and night, putting their very lives on the line while I make dinner or walk the dogs or pour coffee. The obits are the stories of their lives and their accomplishments, which are the greatest and most unselfish of all.

Sacrificing one's life for another.

But not every obit is of a soldier or a famous doctor, and that's precisely the point. Lots of obits are of cooks, dentists, teachers, and mechanics. Every death matters, because every life matters.

Everybody owes somebody, sometime.

For example, I read an obit today about a high school English teacher. I can't imagine how many people owe her. Hundreds, maybe thousands, in all her years of teaching. I also read an obit of a fire captain who trained new firefighters at the fire academy. This was a man who saved lives and taught others to save lives. How many people owe him?

Plenty.

In our own lives, whom do we owe? Mother, father, daughter,

sister, brother, aunt, teacher, doctor, girlfriend. It's all in the obits. Each one tells the story of a human life, and of a family's love. I look at the notices, I see the names. Grieved by grand-children and great-grandchildren. Greatly missed by his father. Survived by a beloved wife.

It sounds simple to say, almost simplistic, but all of us are connected by love and by gratitude.

And the proof, its very particulars, are the obits.

It's true that I'm a little sad after I finish reading them.

Sometimes the pictures break my heart.

The faces smile at the camera, grinning at someone they love, happy and alive.

They're me.

And I remember how lucky I am, every morning.

How lucky we are, in each other.

Past, present, and even future.

All of us.

Amen.

Vroom

~~~

I think I need a new car.

But I'm not sure.

I love my car, and I also love the fact that it's paid for. It's only five years old but it has over 100,000 miles. I know that's a lot, but my friend whose husband is a mechanic said it should go to 200,000. And I'm not being a cheapskate, but I was liking the idea of taking care of something and having it last longer than one of my marriages.

It may not happen.

But as I say, I'm not sure.

It's hard to know if you need a car divorce.

The past few months, lots of things have been going wrong, first with the brakes and then with some kind of pump. The most recent problem was that the entire car began sinking onto its tires. This happened while I was driving, and red lights were flashing like crazy on the dashboard, blinking CAUTION CAUTION CAUTION.

This freaked me out, especially because Daughter Francesca was in the car. You know me well enough to imagine how I'd react to that. Mommy doesn't want a car problem when baby's on board.

Plus she wasn't in her car seat, because she's twenty-four.

The only good news is that this disaster struck while I was near the dealership, so I was able to hobble there before the wheels began trailing smoke like the Batmobile.

It might have been the last straw for me and the car.

The dealer was able to fix it, but the repair was expensive, and it got me wondering, not for the first time. Maybe we really were over. How many things have to go wrong before we call it quits? In other words, I'm unhappy, but am I unhappy enough?

And am I ready to start seeing other cars?

Obviously I've been here before, twice. But ironically, that was a lot easier question, both times. My car worked better than either of my marriages, even considering that it now spontaneously combusts.

If relationships had red lights that blinked CAUTION CAUTION CAUTION, I might not be DIVORCED DIVORCED DIVORCED.

Anyway, I don't know what kind of car I want. I hadn't even begun to go there. I started taking special note of the car commercials on TV, and honestly, all the cars look the same. They drive around mountainsides and avoid squirrels. They have tops and tires. They're all the same car, just with different names.

Then I went online to take a look at what's on the market, like a rookie on match.com. I started with Google, where I plugged in "how to choose a new car," which Google helpfully filled in as "how to choose a new career path."

The only thing dumber than going on Google to choose a new car is going on Google to choose a new life.

Google sent me to websites that made all sorts of suggestions, like "top ten cars for women," "top ten fuel-saving cars," and "top ten deals on wheels." Of these I checked the cars for women, which turned out to be code for minivans.

Uh, no.

I put my nursing bras away, thanks.

I'd been thinking for a long time that I should get a Prius, to help the environment and to feel morally superior.

Twice-divorced people rarely get to feel morally superior.

Then I realized that most of the car companies had "build your own" features, where you could choose a model, color, interior, and options, so I started clicking. I started with Ford, which put me onto Volvo, and on the site, there are like twenty different models, in S, V, X-C, and several other letters, which was dizzying. I switched to Lexus, then to Toyota, then to Mercedes, and two hours later, I had built more cars than a factory.

But I didn't fall in love.

It's all too confusing, this mixing of cars and relationships, and in the end, I rejected the Prius because it doesn't have four-wheel drive.

I need four-wheel drive.

Till death do us part.

Put It in Park

~~~~~~~~~~

I'm back from test-driving three different cars at three different dealerships.

What have I learned?

That eenie meenie miney mo is an excellent way to buy a car.

There are three types of cars in contention: a small sedan, an SUV, and a sport coupe. Most people would narrow down their choices, but these are the three cars I like. Why compare apples to apples when you can compare apples to Snickers?

Any of these cars would meet my need, which is to run errands with at least two dogs. The cavaliers, Peach and Little Tony, always sleep on the passenger side of the front seat, and Penny the golden usually sits in the backseat. Angie stays at home, the Cinderella of dogs, and Ruby makes her clean the fireplace, like the evil stepmother.

Before I started car shopping, I thought that any largish car would do. All cars look the same, and they all get you there. But when I started driving them, I started driving myself crazy.

Now my head is filled with engine volumes, heated seats, drive trains, and special TV cameras for when you reverse. One car has a double visor, another has a retro dashboard clock. In the end, what really matters is that the car is safe and has great cupholders.

To me, a car is a cupholder with an engine.

I brought the brochures home and immersed myself in jargon and dimensions, but that was no fun at all.

Then it struck me. I realized that if I thought of these cars as men, this would be a more interesting decision.

Hmm.

I can do that.

What kind of man is a sedan, an SUV, or a sport coupe?

To begin, the sedan would be the marrying kind of cars. Reliable, dependable, and the sort of car you want to have kids with. A good provider on wheels, but not so boring that it wouldn't notice if you changed your hair color or dropped a few pounds. An even-tempered, keep-it-real guy, but classy enough that you wouldn't have to fib about how much you spent on those shoes.

To sum up, the sedan would be a great husband, which I hear exists and is not yet extinct in certain parts of the world.

I'm liking the sedan, the more I think about it.

I do.

The only problem with the sedan is that I have a sedan now, and the best color offered in the sedan is white, so this would be my fourth white sedan. This is like marrying the same white guy over and over, which is the one mistake I didn't make.

I married two different white guys.

So I feel a little lame choosing the hubbymobile.

After all, I'm still single, and I'm not dead yet.

The second car is an SUV, which I visualize as the Brawny Paper Towel Guy of cars. Not necessarily a hot guy, but a rugged kind of guy, who exists only in romance novels or maybe in Canada.

A manly car.

A car that came with a tool belt.

A car that could build its own garage.

A car that could cut down trees, split wood, and build a fire. This car would smell like hard work and hard soap, and wear a checkered flannel shirt with the sleeves rolled up on muscular forearms. And this car would leave a few buttons open at the neck, not on purpose but just because he was out doing manly things with no coat on, and the open collar would reveal that he had the perfect amount of chest hair.

For chest hair, I don't need cupholders.

I can hold my own cup.

Ahem.

But on the other hand, there are times when I dress up. Not often, but sometimes. And when I'm wearing something nice, I don't want to be seen on the arm of the Brawny Paper Towel Guy of cars.

If he's wearing Timberlands, I can't wear heels.

So he might not be the car guy for me.

The last car choice is the sport coupe, and if you need me to tell you what kind of man the sport coupe is, you're new around here. Sleek, sexy, and fast, this is a superhot, powerful car with a Spanish accent, or maybe French, or Italian. Okay, let's just make it a European accent that renders everything the car says incomprehensible, especially when it whispers in your ear, which is when you realize it doesn't matter what the car said, only that it whispered into your ear.

Vroom vroom.

This car is the kind of man who would get you in trouble with the law.

You could get a speeding ticket standing still in this car, and you might even start stealing other cars if it would make this car happy.

You would perform for this car instead of the other way around.

In short, if I got the coupe, I could end up in jail.

Maybe I should rethink this decision.

And take a cold shower.

Just Desserts

~~~~~~~~

It can be a problem when your kid comes home to visit. You're not used to living together, and even the littlest thing can cause a fuss.

For Daughter Francesca and me, it was dessert.

We're finally on the same page, food-wise, which is a nice way of saying that we're both trying to lose weight, so we're eating healthy foods. She's home this weekend, so for dinner I made politically correct pasta. By which I mean, I sautéed a few tomatoes in olive oil with whole cloves of garlic, and when the mixture got soft, I took it out of the pan and dumped it on top of whole-wheat spaghetti.

By the way, the best thing about this recipe, which I invented, is that it uses garlic without having to chop it up. I hate it when my fingers smell like garlic, and I don't buy garlic already chopped, because that's cheating. But this way, if you toss whole cloves in the pan, they get mushy, and you can mash them with a fork. Mashing is more fun than chopping, and doesn't involve your fingers.

You pay nothing extra for these culinary tips.

Go with God.

And before I tell you about the fight, let me mention also that I'm working on portion control. I know that's my main problem. This should have been a reasonable-calorie dinner, even though it's pasta, but I always up the ante by getting a second and a third helping. You might ask, why do you make so much food in the first place, Lisa? The answer is simple.

I'm Italian.

Actually the truth is, I like to make extra of everything, like scrambled eggs, so I can give some to the dogs. Every morning, I make six eggs, knowing that I'll eat two and give them the rest. They wait patiently during my breakfast, knowing that their eggs will come. It's all very easy.

But I was doing the same thing with whole-wheat pasta, making extra for the dogs, until I realized I was using them as my portion-control beard.

I busted myself and stopped.

To stay on point, I made a delightful spaghetti meal, and Francesca made a side salad. We had a fun dinner, yapping away and trying not to eat more helpings of pasta, even though it was calling to us from the colander. When we finished our meal, I wanted dessert.

This, I can't help.

I love to eat dessert right after dinner. And when I say right, I mean immediately. Timing is everything. It doesn't have to be a lot of something, just a taste. It's not my fault, and I figured out why this is so:

It's because *dessert* sounds so much like *deserve.* Also, we say that people get their *just deserts,* which means they get what they deserve. So, ipso fatso, I feel as if I deserve dessert.

Right now.

But Francesca doesn't like dessert right after dinner. She can wait, which I consider a four-letter word.

This is a long-standing battle we have, because I like us to eat together, and the conversation usually goes like this: I ask her, "Want some dessert?"

She answers, "No, thanks. We just ate."

"But don't you want something sweet? I'm having mine now."

"No, I'm not hungry for dessert yet."

I get cranky. "When do you think you'll want dessert?"

"I don't know. Later."

"Sooner later or later later?"

Okay, so usually I don't eat my dessert then, and we retire to the family room, where we watch TV and work, and I spend the rest of the night asking her, "Is it later yet?"

Just like she used to ask me, "Are we there yet?"

Payback, no?

So last night, I figured I'd solve this problem. All I wanted was a small helping of vanilla ice cream, with a banana. And because I wanted it right after dinner, I decided to have it then. If I had to eat alone, so be it. Plus, this way I'd have more time to burn off the calories, by reaching for the remote throughout the evening.

So I had my ice cream and banana.

Delicious.

But then what happened was that sometime around nine o'clock, Francesca sauntered into the kitchen and returned with a small plate of vanilla ice cream. She strolled over to the couch, sat down, and started eating.

I stared at her, along with the dogs.

It looked so delicious. I could almost taste it on my tongue. In fact, I could taste it on my tongue, because I had it two hours ago.

Two *whole* hours ago.

So you know where this is going.

I had to have a second dessert.

I told her it was her fault, and we had a fight.

In the end, I apologized, because she was right.

And I got what I deserved.

New York Hot Dog

By Francesca Scottoline Serritella

I was walking my little dog, Pip, late the other night, and a young man struck up a conversation that has really stuck in my head. The man happened to be very good-looking, so that could have been part of it, but I digress. He cooed over Pip, and I said proudly, "He's my baby."

The man looked up, flashed me a smile, and asked, "But why would you want that? Now that you have a baby, you can't come get a drink with me."

Cheesy come-on aside, the man has a point. It's not easy being a mother in the city, even if it's only mother to a dog.

I worry about Pip. I know this is not new to all the moms out there, but it's new to me. And there's a lot to worry about in the city. Just last month, a young woman was hit by a cab crossing the street, breaking *both* her legs, but what she was most worried about was her little Yorkie, who had gotten lost in the commotion!

Pip loves to chase pigeons, and I'm always worried he's going to slip out of his lead and chase one into the street. So I bought him a harness that is tough enough for a paratrooper.

I still wish it had an air bag.

And I could never bear to tie him up outside a store, even

for a minute. He's just so cute, he would be too tempting to steal. And he's so friendly, he'd probably trot gaily along with his kidnapper. He'd be the Patty Hearst of dogs.

And I'd be left in the agony of not knowing what became of him, or worse, I'd find him robbing a bank in a floppy hat.

It's too horrible to imagine.

So rather than leave him outside, I put on my best Whadda-you-lookin-at? New Yorker face and march Pip right into the coffee shop and the local bodega. Once inside, his puppy charms do the trick, and no one asks me to leave.

Good dog.

But one time he lifted a leg on the stack of newspapers outside.

Bad dog.

I am a total helicopter mom at the dog park. Instead of sitting on a bench yakking into my phone like most of the dog parents, I trail ten feet behind Pip, keeping a watchful eye on the mastiff lounging—or lying in wait?—and the terrier chewing—a little *too* intensely—his dirty tennis ball.

I don't want Pip falling in with the wrong crowd.

Luckily, Pip is far better socialized than I am. He politely makes the rounds, first of dog butts, then of human knees. With his ever-wagging tail and his big, bright eyes, he is so charming that people often put down their phones or BlackBerrys and actually pull him into their laps. And these are New Yorkers!

The dog should run for office. He'd get three terms, no problem.

But even when he's safe at home, I often worry about leaving him alone too long. Instead of being a café nomad like I was at school, now I write only at home to be with him. And I regularly pass on outings with friends that could keep me out too long. Every potential date has to pass the high bar of being more fun than sitting on the couch, watching TV, and sharing a vanilla yogurt with Pip.

Don't get around much, anymore.

Was it the right choice, getting a dog so soon after moving here?

I think about it, lying in bed. I see Pip has just completed his nighttime bed rotation, a series of sleeping positions and repositions that begin at the foot of my bed and end at my head. My pillow makes a little *pat* sound as he flops his chin on the edge of it, and he gives a tiny snort, the dog equivalent of a satisfied sigh. I stroke the soft fur on his head and watch his chocolate brown eyes grow dozy until his heavy, russet lashes close them for good.

Like I said to the man in the street that night, "He's worth it."

Fictional Blonde

~~~~~~~~~

Daughter Francesca has a theory about ordering in a restaurant, which is to have the meal the way it's offered on the menu. She believes that the chef knows what he's doing, even if we don't, and all the dishes in the meal work together, so we shouldn't mess with what we don't understand. For example, if the salmon is served with lentils, she's not a fan of substituting rice.

Which brings me to my hair.

Because the same reasoning might apply.

Maybe I should've stuck with lentils.

In other words, what if the big chef in the sky made the choice of which color hair goes with my eyes and skin, and I was wrong to start tampering?

Because, bless me, Father, I have tampered like crazy.

I began life with light brown hair that I started highlighting when I was twenty. I used to go with starter blond, which turned out to be a gateway drug, and soon I embarked upon my quest to find the perfect blond. I kept changing the shade visit after visit, trying to find the one that was just right.

I was like Goldilocks, about my goldilocks.

I went through butterscotch to caramel and other delicious

hues, then tried the array of shades that matched the sun at different times of day, from dawn to dusk, like a human sundial.

Bottom line, if it's yellow, it's been applied to my head.

I've been lightening lightened hair for so long that no one knows what my real color is, not even my hair. And lately it's starting to look a little strange. Maybe it's not the best thing to drown your hair with God-knows-what chemicals for several decades?

Not to mention that I'm also going gray, a fact foretold by the few strands I see catching the sunlight, glinting like a shiny chrome fender. Don't get me wrong, I love the chic look of a headful of silvery hair, but I'm not there yet, and the strands sprouting in front of my ears make me look like the Bride of Frankenstein.

Would that make Frankenstein Thing Three?

Anyway, so now when we highlight my hair, we have to account for the gray sections. Plus the outermost sections, dyed sun-drenched blond in the summer of 2008. Also the lowlights underneath, a tawny hue from October 2007. And don't forget the cool ash color I tried in the spring of 2009. All the seasons of my life are laid out in lemony stripes. Sometimes I catch sight of some of my hair, lying on my shoulder, and I don't recognize it as mine.

I don't even recognize it as human.

Of course, I've talked this over with my haircolorist Carol, whom I've been going to for a long time. I want to make clear that none of these crazy ideas were hers. She always advises me against my wackiness, and I have yet to listen. She's an expert at hair color, in addition to life, and she's my girlfriend, therapist, and confessor.

No relationship is closer than haircolorist and fake blonde.

Everyone I know who highlights her hair, and that is everyone I know, tells their haircolorist everything. Carol has gotten me through marriages, book deals, blind dates, doggie deaths, and new puppies. She listens to me whine in my quest for the perfect blond, and at my request, she tweaks the secret formula every visit.

But lately I'm wondering if Francesca's right.

I didn't listen to the chef in the sky.

So maybe it's time to start listening to Chef Carol.

Lost and Found

~~~~~~~~~

Did you ever lose something that you really cared about?

I'm not speaking figuratively, about losing your innocence, or about something important, like losing someone you love. I mean an object, maybe even a small and dumb object, that you lost and really want back.

Like a blue fleece hat.

Which you owned for decades and fit you perfectly and even jingled when you walked.

Yes, I lost my all-time favorite hat. It was soft and perfect, even if it looked funny, which was the point. It was shaped like a court jester hat, with three floppy flaps coming out of the top and a bell on each end. Two of its three bells had fallen off but it was doing fine with the one. It had been washed 384 times but never pilled or lost its bold cobalt color, like a blue M&M for the head.

In short, it was a great hat, and I owned it for twenty-two years.

Tell you how I lost it.

I was walking the dogs, and it was cold enough to wear the hat. Then I got warm, took it off, and stuffed it in my coat pocket. But when I got home, I realized it had fallen out.

At first I thought, no problem. I was sure it would still be on the road where I'd dropped it. I walk around the same block every day, around really pretty farms. The walk is two miles long, and it takes an hour, or one gabby cell phone call. Where I walk, there are only rarely cars. If I see four cars in an hour, that's a lot.

So I hurried back, retracing my steps and dragging the dogs, who whined the whole time because they're big Drama Queens, especially the corgi.

But my hat wasn't on the road anywhere. Or at the curb or in the brush. Only ten minutes later, it was gone.

Noooooo!

Then, there, in the middle of the road with the dogs panting, I flashed on an odd thing that had happened during the walk, earlier that day. A pickup truck had gone past me with two men in the front seat, and the driver was laughing at the passenger, whom I couldn't see. At the time, I'd actually thought, isn't it nice that people are having fun?

Little did I know what they were laughing at.

My hat.

They took my hat! The passenger must have seen it on the road and picked it up, instantly realizing its perfection, as anyone would. And he must have put it on, making the driver laugh, the two of them unable to believe their great good fortune in finding the Hat of the Century.

Of course, later I drove around the block in the car, calling into the wind.

No hat.

I checked for it every time I walked. No hat. I couldn't believe my hat was gone for good. I kept expecting it to turn up. I had entered the first stage of grief.

Denial.

Then I said to myself, you lost your hat, so replace it. But I searched every store and online, and nobody makes it anymore.

Time went by, seasons changed, and I tried to get over it. I thought, you're an adult, so you shouldn't care so much about a dumb hat with only one bell. In fact, find the lesson in it. Learn to let go of hats you love. Get some perspective. I even told myself that the hat, which was magical, made me happy, and now it's making other people happy.

Even if they are BAD people who KEEP THINGS THAT DON'T BELONG TO THEM, which should be a major felony!

The second stage of grief is anger, and boy, was I angry.

The third stage is bargaining, and I couldn't find anyone to bargain with. I suspect that God and Eastern Mountain Sports may have bigger concerns.

The fourth stage is depression but that's no fun at all, so I turned to books for guidance. According to *Bartlett's Quotations,* a guy named Herodotus said, "Of all possessions, a friend is the most precious."

Herodotus misses the point. I have friends, but I still want my hat. A friend can't keep your head warm.

I read a lot of other philosophers, who insist that possessions don't matter and the material world falls away and blah

blah blah. None of them persuaded me. What a bunch of goody-goodies. Didn't they ever lose anything?

Or more accurately, didn't they ever have something TAKEN FROM THEM by MEAN PEOPLE driving around the block?

The final stage is acceptance, but I'm stuck in anger.

And I'm staying here until I get my hat back.

Name Game

~~~~~~~~

I'm a big fan of men. In fact, I'm a major man fan.

But I have a problem, as a woman writer. I've had men tell me they love my books, but they feel funny carrying them around because they have women on the cover.

Or women's legs.

It's time to clear this up. True, the main characters in my books are women, but that's just because I write what I know. It doesn't mean that the books are only for women.

The bottom line for you, dear reader, is that you can just sit back and relax with your reproductive organs, whichever they may be. In fact, more than half of the people who read my books are men.

Smart, cool, handsome, sexy men.

I'm positive that the same is true of the men who read this book. In fact, I can smell the testosterone, welcoming as morning coffee. You're smart, cool, handsome, and incredibly sexy.

Confident enough to know that reading a book by a woman doesn't compromise your masculinity.

Open-minded enough to defect from the biographies and history books on occasion.

Spontaneous enough to appreciate a chuckle now and then.

Real men read me.

Let me tell you a story, to illustrate my point: A few years ago, I found myself in a newsstand at the Atlanta airport while I was on book tour, and I happened to see a man pick up my new book from the rack to decide whether to buy it. I hid behind the candy counter and watched him, waiting to see what his decision would be. Some people might call this stalking, but they don't have my mortgage.

This is what happened: He looked at the cover of my book. He read the inside flap copy about the plot. He skimmed a few pages. He even checked out my author photo on the back. And then he made his decision. He returned the book to the rack.

NOOOOOO! I screamed in my head. I'M REJECTED! I'M A LOSER! AND I PAID TWO HUNDRED BUCKS TO PHOTOSHOP THAT PICTURE!

Then I calmed down.

I thought to myself, What did I do wrong?

There was only one way to find out. So I bought a copy of my own book and brought it to the man in the store.

I said to him: "Excuse me, sir, but I noticed you were looking at this book for a long time. I'm the author and I'd like you to have it, as my gift."

"*You're* the author?" he asked, in disbelief. (I could read between the lines. What he really wanted to say was, *you're* the broad on the back of the book? How can that be? You look nothing like her! And what's up with your roots? Have you been incarcerated?)

"Honestly, I am the author." I signed the book and handed it to him. "But I do have a question. I'm wondering why you didn't buy the book. Would you mind telling me?"

"Okay," he answered. "I didn't buy it because I never buy books by women authors."

Ouch. "Well, I hope you give me a chance and read it. And if you do, please drop me an email and let me know what you think."

Three days later, the man sent me an email, which read: "I really liked your book. You write like a man."

I took it as a compliment.

But in my view, although there are differences between men and women, I'm not sure anybody writes like a man or like a woman. And by the same token, women will like writing by men, and men will like writing by women. I suspect this has to do with the fact that we're sentient human beings. I write for a sensibility, not a gender, and if you like this book, you share that sensibility.

So welcome, gentlemen, and do come again.

If you're man enough.

The Lady Business

~~~~~~~

By Francesca Scottoline Serritella

It's no secret that women compare themselves to each other. The woman running on the treadmill next to me, or sitting across from me in the subway car, or untangling her dog's leash from mine—I can size each one up in a glance—her clothes, her weight, her hair, her makeup. But it's okay, she's doing it to me, too. It's how we get a sense for norms, trends, and where we fit in.

Since I moved to the city, I've observed that women wear sky-high heels and blow-dry their hair straight. I go with the heels thing—it's not so bad, I've developed a minor addiction to Advil and cracking my toes—but I actually like my naturally curly hair, so I let it exist in all its springy, poufy glory. Standing out is okay with me. My hair is my thing.

On my head.

Down south is a different story. I'm a nice girl, a fun girl, a regular girl. Down in nether nether land, I don't want to make a statement. I just want to be normal.

But what is normal? It's the one thing we can't compare with other women by looking at them. Some of my friends spill every dirty detail about their boyfriends' particulars, but we're all too squeamish to discuss our own.

How do you keep up with the Joneses when you have no idea what the Joneses are doing?

Part of the problem is that we can't talk about it. Not that we don't talk about it, but that we can't bring ourselves to say the words. We speak in euphemism: "down there," "bikini area," "hoo-hah."

You know it's bad when Oprah, the richest, most powerful woman in the world, is too embarrassed to call it anything but "va-jay-jay."

Recently, I was talking to two of my closest girlfriends, and the subject of intimate grooming came up. The language barrier was clearly an issue:

"I'm pretty neat, I mean, I take care of myself," my friend said.

"Take care of . . . everything?" I asked.

"Well, almost. I mean, not *everything* everything, but kinda."

My third friend joined in, tentatively. "Really? I just do sort of what matters."

"Matters for what?"

"Oh, you know."

But I didn't know. At that point, I had no idea what we were talking about. And I'm not sure they did either. But we were all too giggly and red-faced to say anything further.

Even the salons are too shy for specifics. The last time I made an appointment, I had three choices: bikini wax, French bikini wax, or a Brazilian. What is a French wax? I thought French women were notorious for not shaving their armpits, now we're putting them in charge of the lady business?

I've heard that the label "Brazilian" is a fiction of marketing; the style did not originate in Brazil at all. How did a perfectly innocent country get such a bad reputation? Did it sleep around with Peru and Colombia?

My mom's favorite joke is, "When did a 'Brazilian' stop being someone from Brazil?"

Actually, my mom thinks the whole thing is pretty funny. Women her age have a different perspective on the issue. She grew up during the sixties, the sexual liberation, and the rise of feminism.

My generation's unifying movement, if we have one at all, is overexposure. Reality TV, Twitter, Facebook, YouTube. The upside is that self-expression can be empowering. But I think the downside is harder on women than men.

Paparazzi rush female stars as they get out of their cars, hoping for a careless exit. Ashton Kutcher tweets a photo of his wife, Demi Moore, in her underwear. Even the squeakiest of clean starlets get tangled in sex-tape scandals, since it takes two seconds for an ex-boyfriend to make the private public.

I can't help feeling like there's a spotlight where the sun-don't-shine. But I guarantee that whatever I do down there . . .

I'm not telling anyone.

A Day At The Opera

We adults don't have enough fun. We go to work and the dry cleaner's. We shop for produce and pet food. We attend the weddings of our cousins and make conversation with people we don't know. We have so many errands and obligations that when we've finally performed them all, we sit around and do nothing, delighted that no one is torturing us anymore.

I know it's easier to do nothing than to do something.

But I suspect it's a big mistake, which could lead to depression and maybe even cellulite.

I drag myself out of my house when I get a Bright Idea to do something fun, just for me. Many of my Bright Ideas suck. Once I bought a bat house that you had to build yourself and paint, which is embarrassing to admit in print. It was an arts-and-crafts project for the menopausal.

I never built it, and my bats remain homeless.

Women of a certain age have no business with glue guns.

One of my more successful Bright Ideas was to go to the Metropolitan Opera—at the mall. You may have read about the Met's program, which telecasts live opera performances to movie theaters. It was way more fun than a bat house. Go. Order tickets online. And don't worry, there are subtitles. Fun subtitles.

It's not like going to a normal movie—it's better. The crowd dresses nicer, as if we were all at the real opera house and not just the multiplex. I share this delusion and wear my contacts for maximum hotness.

Wow!

Before the opera starts, the camera pans the gilded Met balconies, and the real-life orchestra tunes up, a high-rent cacophony. The camera takes you into the orchestra pit, close enough to read the score. The musicians look excited, and the female violinist smiles shyly. I like her instantly. The enormous screen spans the actual stage, so you feel like you-are-there, though you didn't spend-the-money.

The coming attractions roll, for Rossini's *The Barber of Seville* and Puccini's *Il Trittico.* Not your typical Hollywood trailer— nothing explodes, and there are no special effects. At the intermissions, everybody in the audience talks to each other, chattering away in a surprising array of languages. The opera I saw, Tchaikovsky's *Eugene Onegin,* attracted a Russian-speaking crowd. They cried like babies at the end of the show, proving that you don't have to be Italian to lack emotional control.

And they were extraordinarily polite, unlike the couple to my left, who shook their Milk Duds throughout the entire first act, so I had to get all Ricardo Muti on their heinies. *Eugene Onegin* is about unrequited love. The heroine is named Tatiana, sung by Renée Fleming, and she falls for the hunky Onegin, sung by studly Dmitri Hvorostovsky. Tatiana writes Onegin a letter professing her love, sealing wax and all. Onegin spurns her initially, only to come around after she's married.

How do you say "intimacy issues" in Russian?

Onegin borrows also from Tchaikovsky's own life, in which

he received passionate letters from a woman who fell in love with him. But Tchaikovsky was gay.

D'oh!

No matter, he married her anyway and later died an unfortunate death. So neither Onegin nor Tchaikovsky end happily.

But the three-hour production took all of us out of our stupid Saturday errands. We burst into spontaneous applause after the arias, even though Renée Fleming couldn't hear us. We didn't care. We felt like clapping, and we did. I suspect that those endorphins added a year to our collective life span.

And while we watched the opera with the real audience at the Met, something magical happened. A crowd gathered, nationwide, and we all began to feel a part of something larger. Or at least I felt that way and projected it wildly onto everyone else. Like all great art, opera has the power to transport the imagination and to move heart and soul.

So go.

Have fun.

Even next to the Best Buy.

Amoeba

~~~~~~~

Daughter Francesca says I'm an amoeba.

"A what?" I ask. I remember vaguely what an amoeba is, but biology was a long time ago. "Remind me."

"A single-celled organism, immediately affected by a stimulus."

She actually said that sentence.

I don't know exactly what she's talking about, as she went to Harvard, though I get the drift. I'm a happy drunk, and it doesn't take much to get me happy. A half glass of wine, and I'm off and running. A margarita, and I might remarry.

Or get another dog.

I learned this about myself at an early age, when The Flying Scottolines went out to a restaurant, to celebrate something. I forget the occasion but I remember the place, The Frog in Philadelphia, because it was on the classy side for us. Mother Mary wanted everyone on their best behavior and stopped just short of insisting that I wear white gloves.

She actually believed that if you went "in town," you had to wear white gloves.

This was in 1970.

I know.

Anyway, I remember that I was fifteen and I had a sip of my father's martini.

And then I tried to kiss the waiter.

The poor guy couldn't lean over the table without me chasing him with my lips. My father smiled, Mother Mary yelled, and years later, Brother Frank told me that he thought the waiter was cute, too.

So I know that alcohol affects me instantly, even in small amounts. You may think it's my imagination, but I swear it isn't. I'm not the kind of girl who needs liquor to kiss waiters.

Wait. That came out wrong.

So I know not to drink too much wine, but what I didn't realize is that I'm affected by coffee, too. I knew it kept me awake at night, but I've been on deadline for a new book lately, and by coincidence, Francesca's been home visiting. She's the one who pointed it out, one morning after I'd had two cups of coffee and snapped at Ruby The Crazy Corgi.

"She's just barking," Francesca said gently, but I frowned.

"I know but I'm trying to work."

"She doesn't know that."

"Well, she should!" I shot back, and we both looked at each other.

Then it hit me.

I'm a happy drunk, but I'm mean on caffeine.

It's true.

I experimented on myself the next few days, drinking coffee as I worked, and I'm not just more alert on coffee, I'm downright nasty. Cranky. Dare I say it?

Bitchy.

Everything frustrated me. The dogs took too long to go to

the bathroom. The microwave took too long to cook a Boca Burger. The computer took too long to wake up. It needed coffee. They all did.

I was the one who should have gone without.

You may be thinking that it isn't news that caffeine can turn you into a witch, but it was to me, and anyway, that's not the point. Because what bothers me is, what does that say about me, if I'm mean on caffeine?

I always enjoyed knowing that I'm a happy drunk, because I believed that it said something about me, inside. The theory is that liquor lets down your inhibitions, showing the real you, and if that was so, it was proof positive that I was a nice person inside.

Generous, sweet, and kind, if lecherous to men in aprons.

But is that still true if I'm mean on caffeine?

Does this new fact show that I'm really evil inside, or at best, have a high-octane dark side?

I don't know.

I'm afraid to ask me.

I might bite.

The Sixth Sense

I've been reading a lot in the news about Ponzi schemes and swindlers like Bernie Madoff, and I feel sorry for the people who were duped. There, but for the money, go I.

I have a friend who says she wouldn't fall for a swindler because she has an excellent you-know-what detector.

I don't. I would have given Bernie Madoff everything I had. My you-know-what detector doesn't detect you-know-what.

Come to think of it, after two divorces, my you-know-what detector might be on the fritz. I'm starting to wonder if it ever worked at all. Honestly, I don't think I even got one in the first place.

Maybe I was behind the door when they gave out the you-know-what detectors. Or my you-know-what detector was doing God-knows-what at the time.

I guess the only protection against people like Bernie Madoff is to rely on your senses, but for me, that's like bringing a knife to a nuclear war. If my senses were my guide, I'd be up the creek without a bank account.

Let's review. There are five senses: sight, smell, hearing, taste, and touch, plus a sixth sense only I have, namely, the knack for arriving at the store just after the sale is over.

We begin with sight.

I couldn't tell just by looking that Bernie Madoff was dishonest. On the contrary, the first time I saw his picture on the news, with his silvery hair and shy smile, his cute baseball cap and black quilted jacket, I thought to myself:

That guy is hot.

Then I checked his left hand, and of course, he was married. Even the cheaters are married. By all accounts, his wife is his college sweetheart and they were very happy together. So he stole from the poor, but he's a great husband.

You have to compromise in marriage.

So I hear.

I couldn't smell Bernie Madoff coming, even though I have the biggest nose in the universe, because my sense of smell is wacky. I love the scent of fresh basil, and I buy only orange-scented detergent because it's green, if you follow. I own fifteen different perfumes for my multiple personalities, and I'm in a bad mood if I'm wearing Creed when I should be wearing Shalimar.

That said, my house smells like wet dogs, and I don't mind it at all. It's not that I don't smell it, it's that I like the smell. If you could put that smell in a fancy bottle, I'd probably wear it instead of Obsession.

Mine is not a nose that could detect a Bernie Madoff. For that, you might need a crime-stopping bloodhound like McGruff.

My sense of hearing is equally unreliable. For example, some evil person gave my computer a virus, so I got a new one, which I hate. The new computer is so loud I can't even think. It has a fan in the back that whirrs like a wind tunnel, and whenever I try to write, all I hear is the stupid fan. I won't even work in my office anymore because I hate the fan so much.

But, at the same time, I work with the TV or the satellite radio on, and sometimes with both. I also live with five dogs, four of whom are barking at any given time, and the fifth is always growling at a cell phone, which is ringing.

None of these sounds bothers me. The computer, I want to throw out the window. So I would've been a sucker for Bernie Madoff's sweet, sweet words, especially the part where he was going to make me rich.

My sense of taste would be useless, because that's good only for detecting chocolate cake, and my sense of touch is notoriously out of touch.

What sense is left?

Common sense.

And nobody has that, where money is concerned.

Risqué Business

~~~~~~~~~~

I was driving along the highway the other day and saw one of those signs naming the group or business that "adopted" the highway, which I guess means they pay to maintain it, but that doesn't matter for this story. What matters is I was driving on a highway adopted by Club Risqué.

I suspected immediately that Club Risqué was not a book club.

When I got home, I plugged Club Risqué into Google and learned that Club Risqué is a "gentleman's club," which is a euphemism for a strip club.

Gentlemen is a euphemism for *horndog*.

On the Club Risqué webpage, there are pictures of women in black thongs, platform shoes, and of course, their birthday suits. In one of the pictures, the women are hugging and kissing.

Maybe they're just good friends.

In any event, it does pose the question—How do we feel about strip clubs adopting our highways?

Surely we can find better parents.

I think even Octomom would be a better parent, though she might have her hands full with the side streets.

Generally, I see the names of insurance companies, car

dealerships, and Boy Scout troops on those highway adoption signs. In other words, a normal business. Do we feel better when a normal business maintains our highways? Or do we prefer a risqué business?

Maybe it's not strange to have all that asphalt paid for by naked dancing. We sure do need to maintain our highways. So I guess we should hope that more and more gentlemen go to strip clubs, and more and more women strip for money. That way, we could have highways all over the place. It would be like the New Deal, only with pornography.

Fun!

FYI, the Club Risqué website says that it used to be known as Dangerous Curves. Good move, changing the name. Dangerous Curves is not a good name for a highway.

Now that I think about it, I might be in favor of a strip club adopting a highway. Their money is as good as anybody else's, and we don't make value judgments about where cash comes from these days, when our biggest growth industry is casino gambling. Every time I open the newspaper, somebody's arguing in favor of building a new casino somewhere. We have casinos at the beach and in the suburbs, and when we run out of land to gamble on, we move to boats and barges. I bet if we ever colonize the moon, right after we plant the American flag, we build the first lunar casino. And then we use the flag for pole dancing.

Flagpole dancing!

Gentlemen would love that!

Just for fun, I went to the Club Risqué webpage for employment opportunities, which advertises jobs for "couch and table dancing." Good news, in these troubled economic times. I would apply right away if my couch or table danced. Instead, my furniture just sits there, slacking off.

My couch is a couch potato.

The website also advertises "champagne courts," though I have no idea what that is. I've been in federal court and state court, but that's not the same thing. I'm guessing there's no law in champagne court, although I bet there's a lawyer or two.

Or seventy-five.

You'll be happy to know that Club Risqué also needs Shot Girls. I hadn't realized that pouring liquor into a shot glass required special skills, but maybe it does. Those glasses are really really small, and the clubs are really really dark. You could spill if you're not careful. So it's good to know that there are plenty of jobs available for skilled women these days. We may not be able to become President of the United States, but we can still pour drinks. For men. Nude.

Whew!

Finally, the website posted jobs for "entertainers" and specified that there was "no funny money."

Maybe that's what Club Risqué used for the highway. Funny money.

Same as Congress.

A Good Girl Is Hard To Find

By Francesca Scottoline Serritella

I know most single girls my age are looking for Mr. Right, and though I'd love to have a boyfriend, you know what I'm really looking for?

Miss Right.

I'd even settle for Miss Right Now.

I haven't switched sides, and I'm not arguing a man's case, I'm talking about platonic relations, a girlfriend, a gal pal, a friend.

All my life, I have been a girl's girl. I grew up as an only child on the hunt for sisters.

Easier said than done.

My mom loves to tell the story of when I started kindergarten, she'd spy on me during recess, and for the first week she saw me walking the perimeter of the school yard singing to myself.

No wonder I had no friends.

I remember the day I summoned the courage to ask a little girl in my class, "Wanna be my best friend?" It was the scariest moment of my young life, if you don't count the part in *The Wizard of Oz* when the monkeys fly out of the witch's castle.

Those monkeys were messed up.

But it worked! I made my first friend. When you're five, a line like that is all you need.

School made it easy. All through high school, I was blessed with a group of five close girlfriends. It got a little tougher in college, but I was still surrounded by girls my age. Now that we've all graduated, my old friends are scattered, and I'm on my own in the great, wide world.

So much of a girl's attention is given to how to meet a man, no one tells us how to meet a friend.

Where do you go to meet girls? I should know the answer, seeing that I am one. But prowling for potential friends requires new territory. You can't go to the places where you'd try and meet a guy. I can't meet a girl at a bar, for example. Well, I could, but she might think I was hitting on her. Or worse, she might view me as competition for guys.

There's no getting close to a girl when her claws are out.

If one thing unites all womankind, it's got to be body insecurity. So I joined a gym, hoping to make some girlfriends.

Total bust.

Turns out, most of the members at my gym are men. With the few women that are there, it's hard to strike up a conversation. We're all plugged into our headphones or absorbed in heavy reading, like *Us Weekly.*

When it comes to Team Aniston vs. Team Jolie, friendships are broken, not made.

Women talk in the locker room, but only to people who are already their friends. Nudity is not the ideal icebreaker.

"Yowza, did that tattoo hurt?"

Awkward.

Anyway, I spend most of my time in the locker room with my eyes to the ground, trying not to look. For everyone's comfort, clothed interactions are best.

But what to wear? You have to dress well for a girl. We want fashionable friends, preferably our same size so we can borrow clothes.

But you can't be too dressed up, either. Nothing turns a woman off more than a girl who "thinks she's all that." You want to attract a man? Show some cleavage. You want to attract a female friend? Wear adorable ballet flats. When she comments on your shoes, start griping about how much heels hurt.

Complaining is the glue of female friendships.

My mother is always trying to set me up on playdates with her friends' daughters. I appreciate the effort, but it's not so easy to cold-call a girl.

Men, I don't know how you do it.

Although I think the stakes are even higher when courting someone for friendship. If I flirt with a guy and he blows me off—whatever, maybe I wasn't his physical type. But if I'm trying to forge a friendship with a girl and she rejects me, it's much more personal. I can't blame it on pheromones or something superficial.

She didn't like me for me.

Feeling discouraged, I did what I always do to clear my head: I took my dog, Pip, for a walk. Outside, the laughter of a group of girls caught my attention, and I hardly felt Pip pulling at the leash to meet a black dog coming toward us. Soon, Pip's tail was wagging so hard that his entire body wiggled, so I let him engage in some butt-sniffing.

"I think our dogs are friends," said the woman holding the other leash. "Is this Pip?"

"Yeah, it is." I looked up, surprised, and noticed that the girl looked familiar.

"We've seen you in the neighborhood before. This is—"

"Pepper!" I remembered.

"Right. I'm Carolyn. I always learn the dogs' names but not the people's."

"I'm the same way. I'm Francesca."

And I might be your new friend.

Story Time

~~~~~~~

Once upon a time is one of my favorite phrases in the world. Also, *a man walks into a bar.* Why? Because they begin a story.

I love to hear a good story. Everybody does. Maybe it started with a story told around a campfire, or a bedtime story told in your childhood room, with the outside world at bay.

I love to tell stories, too. I tell a story every year in a novel and plenty more at the dinner table. Lots of people like to tell stories, and it's the same instinct whether it's me talking or your best friend. Authors are just storytellers with a royalty rate.

Stories hold a power all their own. Think of Scheherazade, telling stories so good they saved her life. Or the thousands of fables and legends that have lasted through centuries. They answer a primal need to know about each other, to learn from each other, and to talk to each other.

And as we know, a story has a beginning, a middle, and an end. A story without an ending is like a sentence without a punctuation point. In my view, that's what happened to *The Sopranos.* The story stopped, but it didn't end, and they're not the same thing. The promise of once-upon-a-time is that there will be a they-lived-happily-ever-after, or at least, they-all-got-whacked. The fact that so many *Sopranos* viewers got angry at its ending proves the power of a story. It didn't matter to them that Tony Soprano was fictional. They still wanted to know what happened to him.

Sadly, *The Sopranos* was the only TV show I watched, and now it's gone. There are no good stories on TV anymore; I mean normal, scripted shows like the ones I loved. *Sex and the City. Seinfeld.* Going farther back, I adored *M*A*S*H* and *The Mary Tyler Moore Show.* Those stories got people talking to each other the next morning around artifacts known as watercoolers. Starbucks would do, too; no matter what the beverage, we'd all gab about the story we'd seen on TV the night before.

But now TV isn't about story, but contest. Who is the best singer? Who the best inventor? Best chef? Dress designer? Men compete for women; women compete for men. We watch game shows, or shows about real lives, but reality TV is the antithesis of fiction and it has hijacked story.

So what happens to a popular culture without story?

Paris Hilton.

At the same time that story has disappeared, gossip has exploded on TV and in newspapers, magazines, and blogs. I think these two things are related. Lindsay Lohan, Britney Spears, and Nicole Ritchie have become our fictional characters. Angelina and Brad have replaced Edith and Archie; Tom and Katie took over from Lucy and Ricky.

Jennifer Aniston is the new Rachel Green.

Celebrities are our heroes and heroines now, discussed the next day over latte or lunch. We have such a strong need to talk to each other, to have some commonality of story, that we're finding it in celebrities. In effect, we're turning reality into fiction. Using actors and actresses, just off duty.

The plotlines of our celebrity characters tend to fall into a pattern—how the mighty have fallen—but that's still juicy. They marry and divorce. They go to rehab and come out again. The paparazzi have become our new storytellers.

Some of the celebrity stories have unhappy endings, but mostly they go on and on. Next week there's a new episode, like an arc in a plotline. The characters reproduce, shave their heads, get tattoos. Sometimes they get their tattoos on *Miami Ink* or buy a Harley customized on *American Chopper,* and we can watch that, too.

And if it's not too meta to follow, sometimes the celebrities fictionalize themselves in a reality series. In *The Sarah Silverman Show,* the comedienne employs her real-life sister to play themselves in a scripted storyline. Tori Spelling fictionalized herself in NoTORIous. We've got plenty of actors, but no spare parts.

And how is this working for us? Not great.

It leaves us with a perennially empty feeling. We find the celebrities empty, and at some level, we find ourselves empty for paying them so much attention. We've become reluctant voyeurs, and at some level, we know they're just people trying to live their lives. It hurts them, and it hurts us, too. Our culture begins to lack content, depth, and substance. We miss the richness of human experience that story embodies, reflects, and carries forward.

We might have to go back to reading books.

Yay!

Hairy, The Sequel

I used to have only two dogs, golden retrievers, and everybody would ask me if they shed.

Answer? Yes.

I still have the goldens, plus now there are two Cavaliers and a corgi, but nobody asks me if the dogs shed.

Why?

It's obvious.

I'm wearing the answer.

I'm covered with dog hair, all the time. It's stuck on my T-shirts. It weaves itself into my sweatpants. My sweaters have sweaters of their own.

I read recently about this woman who makes sweaters from dog hair, and I would avoid her at all costs. The last thing I need is a dog-hair sweater. A dog-hair sweater covered with dog hair is redundant, at best.

On the plus side, I'm warm at all times, even in coldest winter. When I have a hot flash, I could spontaneously combust.

I'm not complaining, merely observing. If you're the kind of person who acquires five dogs, you're not the kind of person who worries about looking neat as a pin. It ain't gonna happen.

And you can only lint-roll so often. I don't even bother

when I have a book signing, because my beloved readers have come to expect some degree of dishevelment in me, and I do not disappoint. On the contrary, I feel that dog hair adds to my credibility.

I write not only what I know, but what I wear.

I lint-roll only on the rare occasion when I have a date, because then I'm trying to act like something I'm not.

Sane. Clean. Superbly in control.

Take the actress Catherine Zeta-Jones. I read recently that she said something like, "Dogs and children belong in their own bed."

Men love Catherine Zeta-Jones.

I'm not like her.

I think children, dogs, and cats belong in my bed, along with a great book, a box of piping-hot pizza, and a cold Diet Coke. Maybe some chocolate cake, too. Also *The Godfather* on TV.

Dog-hair party!

And dog hair blankets not only my clothes, but my couch, chairs, and rugs. I buy quilted covers that sit on top of the furniture and are supposed to protect it from dog hair and muddy paws, and I even had the covers personalized with THE GIRLS, RUBY, and LITTLE TONY.

But they should read DOG HAIR, MORE DOG HAIR, and DOG HAIR, THE SEQUEL.

Also they have to be moved every time you want to sit down, which gets old. So sometimes I end up leaving the covers on the floor, where the dogs go sit on them, covering them with dog hair. I regard this as efficient. Why should the dogs have to climb on the couch to shed?

Also, this way, I can get dog hair on the cover and the couch at the same time, because we both know that the dogs are going to climb up next to me on the couch, to watch the big TV.

The only thing I don't love is when I find dog hair in the kitchen, or on a plate. And I admit it, this happens. When I cook, sometimes a dog hair on my sleeve will fall into the pan and I have to get it out with a fork. It puts me off my food, right there in the kitchen.

And the other day I had to pick a dog hair off my lip. It was long and yellow, so it had to be one of the goldens'.

You know it's bad when you can identify which dog's hair it is.

Then somebody gave me a plate and a matching mug that reads Everything Tastes Better With Dog Hair.

It's a really cute gift, but I disagree. And I actually know.

So I sat down on my couch, went onto my laptop, and ordered a special pet vac made by Black & Decker. Peach sat beside me, eyeing the screen with concern.

I looked down and gave her a pat, which was when I saw it, on her head.

A long strand of fake-blond hair clung to her ear.

Gotcha.

Library Slut

I'm a library slut.

I visit libraries every year, speaking and fundraising, and nothing gives me greater pleasure than to know librarians and support public libraries.

I'll tell you why.

I owe them.

I wouldn't be an author, or a bookaholic, without libraries.

Mother Mary hates it when I say this, but I grew up in a household with lots of love and meatballs, but only one book.

No, not the Bible.

You know my mother better than that.

The book was *TV Guide*.

Imagine my surprise when I got older and learned that not all books had Lucille Ball on the cover.

I discovered my love of reading in my school library, where the notion of a whole roomful of books seemed extraordinary. That librarian saw that I was a nascent bookworm and sent me home one day with a list of local libraries, and my father took me to all of them.

He waited in the car like a dog. There was no TV in the library.

Of course, once inside, I had no idea how to choose a book and was way too scared to ask anyone. But there were some books that had a picture of a man in profile on the spine, and the man had a big nose like my Uncle Rocky.

And me.

All of The Flying Scottolines have nice, big noses. Mother Mary likes to say that we get more oxygen than anyone else.

She's right. If I'm breathing, you're dead.

Anyway, because of his nose, the man on the spine felt like family, so his were the books I checked out and read like a fiend. Like our girl crush, Nancy Drew.

Only later did I find out that the man wasn't Uncle Rocky, but some guy named Sherlock Holmes.

Who isn't even Italian.

Bottom line, that's why I'm a mystery writer today.

There was another way I chose my library books, then. When I was little, the card in back of the books stayed with the same book, so I used to slide the card from its tight manila pocket and look at the card to see how many people had checked out the book. If there were a lot of signatures, I'd choose that book.

Not the worst method, in a way. It may have been the low-tech equivalent of a bestseller.

But my favorite thing about the library was my library card. It was the first piece of grown-up ID that I got, and it felt like a veritable ticket to adulthood. I carried it proudly in a padded Barbie wallet that otherwise held only a photo of Troy Donahue.

You might have to look him up.

The Troy Donahue photo came with the wallet, from the days when wallets came with photos. Nowadays, you're on your own. Your wallet has no friends.

But to stay on point, I will never forget my library card. It was small, stiff, and orange, and it bore my name in full. LISA MARIA SCOTTOLINE. Next to my name was a metal plate embossed with four numbers. I used to go home and press my finger against the numbers on the metal plate, which were freshly inked from my library trip.

Believe it or not, my numbers were 3937.

How do I remember that, when I can't remember where I put my car keys?

Simple.

Any memory lasts when it's linked with an emotion, and the library card meant the world to me. Its message was clear:

I read, therefore, I matter.

It gave me an identity, as a reader. It told me that others valued what I valued. That I wasn't alone, like some weirdo bookworm.

It's a powerful message, one that I got loud and clear. And it's a message that librarians and libraries give every day, without knowing it, to children and to adults everywhere around the world.

That's why I love libraries.

Librarians, I owe you.

And I'm yours.

A Picture Saved

~~~~~~

Daughter Francesca has grown up and moved away, but I still have plenty of reminders of her here, at the house.

And lately I'm wondering if plenty is too many.

Like any kid, she produced tons of stuff in school—stories, worksheets, poems, French essays, math problems, and countless drawings, from starter rainbows to crayoned self-portraits to pictures of our dogs, cats, guinea pigs, and a bunny named Pee-wee. She brought all the drawings home, where I made a fuss over each, and the ones I didn't hang on the refrigerator door, I put away in a cardboard box. I couldn't bring myself to throw them away.

Especially not while she was watching.

Then I forgot about them, and a habit was born. When one box filled up, I scribbled the year on it and got another, then another, and I'd put them away somewhere, and before I knew it, I had saved almost everything Francesca produced in elementary, middle, and high school.

I still have it all, boxed and labeled, upstairs in the attic.

I've never done anything remotely as organized, before or since.

I'm hoping this doesn't sound dumb, or obsessive, though of

course I'm crazy about my kid and I'm glad I saved a lot of this stuff. For example, I remember when she was getting ready to go off to college and she was really worried. I thought back to her first day of elementary school and went digging in the boxes. Amazingly, I was able to find, in the 1993 box, a drawing she had made, which showed me kissing her good-bye on our porch. Under the picture, she had written in a childish printing:

"Before the first day of school I was a nervus reck. Wen the day came I just said everything is gowing to be ok."

Cute, huh?

She spells better now.

Anyway, that night, I taped her drawing to her bathroom mirror, so she saw it when she woke up on the morning she was going to leave for college. And with it, I wrote her a note that said:

"This is how you'll know you'll be okay at college. Because ten years ago, you were afraid of the first day of school, and everything was okay."

Aww.

Now that's the kind of moment savers live for. It made her happy, it made me happy, and all because I had a drawing from almost forever ago.

But I still have the stuff, and lots of other stuff besides. I saved her clothes because I kept thinking I'd give them away, and in her bedroom is almost every toy or stuffed animal she was ever given.

But it makes me think.

How much do you save of your kid's stuff?

How long do you save it for?

And why can't I part with it now, after I've parted with her?

I went into her old bedroom the other day, mainly to find the cat, and I started looking around, at all the things on the shelves. Each one is a memory. Breyer horses she got from me, a stuffed Jiminy Cricket from Mother Mary, and a photo of her with my father, now deceased, both of them leaning on our old VW station wagon.

What to keep, and what to throw away?

Keep the photo, sure, but the Jiminy Cricket matters as much. And those plastic Breyers aren't going anywhere.

I eyed her dresser, which was covered by a fine layer of dust. And on top of her jewelry box lay something I didn't know she had:

A stack of index cards on which I had drawn cartoons. I used to slip them into her lunch to make her laugh, in middle school. I picked them up and flipped through them.

She had saved every one.

The Nest Isn't Empty, It Just Has More Closet Space

I've written a lot about what it's like to have Daughter Francesca out of the house, and about how much I miss her, and all of it's true. But if this collection proves anything, it's that time changes things. I used to be in a sort of motherly mourning.

Now, well, I'm a merry widow.

Not exactly, but at times.

The bottom line is, being an empty nester isn't the worst thing in the world.

Let me tell you why.

To begin, let's review. I'm a single mother and have been most of my life. So for about twenty years, I've had sole responsibility of a certain little human being. But the truth is, married or no, every mother relates to her child as if she has sole responsibility, because responsibility for a child is something that we carry in our hearts.

All mothers are single mothers, inside.

Proof is, even if a hubby or caretaker is feeding our kid, we know when it's time for her to eat. We know when she gets sleepy, we know when she's waking up. We know that if her nose was sniffly that morning, then it will be worse by four o'clock, too late to get a doctor's appointment. We're always keeping a mental clock of what her day is like. We're always thinking about our children, no matter what we're doing, like tape that runs in the back of our minds, on a continuous loop in our brains.

Call it the mommy lobe.

That's the stuff of our bond. We're connected to our children, all the time, the same as if the cord were still there, a twisted strand of flesh and lifeblood, thick as a jump rope.

I'm sure that there are plenty of dads who feel the same way, and whose brains play the same tape. I think my father did, or at least I felt he did.

But I have ovaries, and I write what I know.

So if you've had this responsibility all your adult life, or at least as far back as you can remember, it gets pretty hairy when your baby bird flies the coop, even though that's been inevitable since she poked through the egg. It feels as if your very reason for being suddenly drops out. I know it seems obvious, but I've lived it, and it wasn't so apparent to me until I did.

Well, I'm happy to report that the nest isn't empty, it just has more closet space.

In other words, there are distinct advantages to being the only one at home. And I'm living that, too, so I can tell it to you. If you're worried or sad about letting your child go, whether it's to kindergarten or to college or to halfway around the world, it's going to be all right. Because one day, you're going to realize that you have a lot more room for your shoes.

And bags.

And sheets, and towels.

And there are other advantages, even delights. When you come back into a room, it will look exactly the way you left it. There won't be open cabinet doors that need closing, or sticky jelly on the counter that needs cleaning, or a dirty milk glass in the sink, which needs to be put in the dishwasher. No cotton balls saturated with nail polish remover that stink up the bathroom, and no wet towels left on the bed. And no sneakers to trip over in the dark, unless that's the way you leave yours, which I totally get.

Hello, your life just got a whole lot easier.

Hallelujah!

Even if your kid was neat, and Daughter Francesca was pretty good in this department, they didn't leave things the way you wanted it. They didn't do things the way you would have.

They're not you.

That's what their declaration-of-independence rants were all about, when you used to fight, and why they kept telling us they want to do it their way.

Well, now, I get to do it my way.

I get to eat what I want when I want, and for me, that can mean cereal for dinner, or just broccoli. Sometimes if I have a big lunch, I have dessert for dinner. I scarf down my favorite ice cream, and there's always enough because nobody eats it but me.

And you know what?

It's fun!

I can stay up late if there's something I want to watch on TV, or I want to finish reading the next chapter in a book. I can work around the clock for three days, then sleep late on the fourth. I can walk the dogs or not, I can go to the movies or not, I can do anything I damn well please.

It's called freedom.

And I earned every minute of it.

And that's the best feeling in the world.

To me, that's our long-delayed reward for decades of hands-on parenting. And for the tape running through the backs of our minds, in mommy lobe, for the rest of our lives.

Whether your nest is full or just has more closet space, I hope you enjoyed this book.

Because it's really about being a woman at the wheel.

We're always moving ahead.

Enjoy the trip.

Acknowledgments

This entire book is an acknowledgment of the gratitude and love that Francesca and I feel for our family, our friends, and each other, but if there are any words worth repeating, they're Thanks and Love.

So here goes.

Thanks and love to the great people at *The Philadelphia Inquirer.* This book was inspired by our "Chick Wit" column, and we're proud that we appear in their newsprint every Sunday. Special thanks to editor Sandy Clark, as well as publisher Brian Tierney, Bill Marimow, Ed Mahlman, and Hilary Vadner.

Big thanks and love to Jennifer Enderlin, our terrific editor at St. Martin's Press, as well as to the brilliant and fun team led by the fearless John Sargent, as well as Sally Richardson, Matt Baldacci, Matthew Shear, Jeff Capshew, Alison Lazarus, Michael Storrings, John Murphy, John Karle, Monica Katz, and Sara Goodman. We appreciate so much your enthusiasm for this book and its predecessor, and we thank you for your hard work, energy, and good humor.

Thanks so much and love to Mary Beth Roche, Laura Wilson, and the other great folks at St. Martin's audiobook division. It was so much fun to record both audiobooks, and we even won an Audiofile Award! These people make even a Philadelphia accent sound good.

Many thanks and much love to our amazing agents, Molly Friedrich, Paul Cirone, and Lucy Carson of the Friedrich Agency. They were all early believers in these books and in us, and they're the smartest, funniest, and most loyal bunch you'll ever meet. God bless them for their great good hearts.

One of the biggest hearts in creation belongs to Laura Leonard, who shepherds every manuscript through publication and shepherds us through life. We don't breathe without consulting Laura, and her friendship sustains us every day. We love you, Laura! And we love Franca Palumbo, who is simply an angel with a slammin' body.

Brother Frank, Francesca, Mother Mary, and Lisa. Welcome to the family.

Of course, family is the heart of this book, because family is the heart of everything. Francesca and I have always valued our bond and felt grateful for Mother Mary's continued health and Brother Frank's continued hijinks. We still miss the late Frank Scottoline, but he is with us always. Writing this book has given us a unique opportunity to laugh at ourselves and to cherish the gift of having three generations of women who truly are best friends.

We suspect we aren't alone in our great good fortune.

Finally, we want to acknowledge our readers. We knew we were lucky before we wrote this book, but by sharing our stories, and by meeting the mothers and daughters, brothers and sisters, fathers and sons who have connected to something we've written here, we have been able to *feel* it. And for that, we extend our sincerest thanks and love to each of you.

Because you're family now, too.